CANDLES, CARTS & CARBOLIC

Candles, Carts & Carbolic

James Callaghan

edited by

Jennifer Callghan

Copyright © Jennifer Callaghan, 2011

First edition, 2011

Published by Palatine Books,
an imprint of Carnegie Publishing Ltd
Carnegie House,
Chatsworth Road,
Lancaster, LA1 4SL
www.carnegiepublishing.com

ISBN 978-1-874181-87-3

Designed and typeset by Carnegie Book Production
Printed and bound in the UK by Short Run Press, Exeter

Contents

Glossary

aft	towards the rear
black gang	crew working in the stokehold of a ship
bloaters	salted herring
blocker man	foreman (a manager down the docks and in the ship repair yards. A foreman wore a trilby type of hat)
bombazine	stiff fabric, usually black and worn as mourning clothes
coke	kind of coal
conny-onny	condensed milk, eaten on bread
coggy	watchman, guard
curry-comb	comb with metal teeth for combing horses
dandy-brush	brush with stiff short bristles used for grooming horses
diddy	short ('diddy' first used about 1805)
dropsy	edema, from congestive heart failure
dowseys	look-out men
Exy-cosher	newspaper delivery boy
farrier	man who shoes horses
feller	man, or boyfriend, husband
fingerposts	signposts, usually in the countryside
forrard	forward
gansey	jumper, pullover, sweater
Heath Robinson	complicated device with a simple function
Hooch	alcohol
Hooray Henry	rather useless upper-class man
jack	policeman, man, fellow
jankers	official punishment for a breach of discipline in the armed forces

jigger	alleyway or passageway at the back of a house
johnnies	sailors
judy	woman, girlfriend (as in 'me judy')
knickerbockers	men's or boys' baggy knee trousers
lairage	temporary storage for livestock at the docks
the Lanny	the landing stage at the pier head
Lascar	sailor from India
lekkies	(electric) trams
legless	drunk
mangle	wringer: machine for pressing wet clothes made of two rollers, operated by turning a wheel
marmalize	beat
midden	rubbish tip
moke	donkey
neatsfoot	oil used to clean and nourish leather. 'Neat' comes from the old name for cattle
nippies	waitresses at Lyons' teashops
the oller	patch of wasteland where children played games or men played 'toss.'
on tick, or 'the weekly'	on credit, also known as 'the never.' Payments were usually collected at the door.
over the brush	unmarried couple living together
paralytic	drunk
parkie	park-keeper
piss-stone	urinal
pogged	punished, beaten
proddy dogs	Catholic taunt for Protestants
provender sacks	sacks for oats and hay
sagging	playing truant
setts	square paving-stones, similar to cobble-stones
shippon	cowshed or barn

side	meanness or hypocrisy. The opposite is: He's got no side on him.
slack	small coal pieces left after coal has been screened
sleveen	a creepy or untrustworthy individual
snug	a small, private room with access to the bar. Ladies would often enjoy a private drink in the snug in a time when it was frowned upon for ladies to be in a pub.
sprogs	a recruit just out of training
tallyman	the man who collected payments at the door for things bought 'on tick'
tanning	the process where animal skins were turned into leather
tanyards	where tanning took place
togee	lumps of brown sugar, usually picked up from the back of Tate and Lyle's sugar refinery
trimmer	man who distributed coal on a steamship
wagging	playing truant
wide boy	man who will use any means to make money
wynds	narrow path snaking through the houses
Zeppelin	airship used in early 20th century for bombing raids

Coins no longer in use:

fudges	farthings
megs	halfpennies (ha'pennies)
wonners	pennies
joeys	threepenny bits
tanners	sixpences
bobs	shillings

Acknowledgements

This book would not have come into being without a lot of support.

I would like to thank my friend Marjorie Gann here in Toronto, Canada for all her patient encouragement and advice through the process of getting this onto the printed page. Thanks also to my friend poet Ruth Pierson (who one day found me hunched over a laptop in a nearby coffee shop, struggling to punctuate 50,000 words) for her belief in my ability to do this. My appreciation to Laurie Lewis of Codger Press, Kingston, Ontario who, in a posada in Mexico, showed me how to download software that would get this dog-eared typewritten script into the computer in editable form and who encouraged me to believe this project was worth completing. Thank you especially to Joan Pierce of Hebden Bridge Yorkshire for all her enthusiasm and interest. John H.G.Archer, architectural historian at the Manchester School of Architecture, encouraged me in my efforts to bring a bit of history back to life.

I appreciate the help of Margaret Greenwood, formerly editor of the National Museums and Galleries on Merseyside website, in showing me where to look for the photos and to Roger Hall, indefatigable archivist at Liverpool Record Office for providing them. Colin Wilkinson of Bluecoat Press Liverpool allowed us to use photographs from his wonderful site, streetsof liverpool.co.uk

I am extremely grateful to Cheryl Dunn, of Shelfstealer digital books for her publishing and legal knowhow which she generously shared with me over a coffee in San Miguel de Allende, Mexico.

Acknowledgements also to the contributors to the forum of Scottie Press, a website for former residents of Scotland Rd. for help with finding the meanings of many of the Liverpool words in the Glossary.

Thank you to Carnegie Publishing: Alistair Hodge for seeing the potential in this book and to editors Anna Goddard and Kate McKellar for their patience and creativity in getting it into shape.

Of course, the greatest acknowledgements must be to my father Jim Callaghan who had the perseverance in the face of all obstacles to complete this book. It is a great pity that he could not be alive still to see it in print.

And to my daughter Anita Sinclair, my greatest supporter.

Introduction

Candles, Carts & Carbolic is Jim Callaghan's story of his early life. Born a hundred years ago, in 1911, he grew up in the working-class, Irish-Catholic neighbourhood of Scotland Road in Liverpool. 'We didn't have any money problems,' he says, writing of the kids he grew up with, 'we had none.' Life was tough, but children knew how to make their own entertainment. As he says, 'Away from school, pain-racked fingers and demoniacal teachers, we lived our young lives to the full.' He played ollies, skipped lekkies and fished in grids for lost coins, all the time at the mercy of the fearful powers around him – the police, the church, school teachers, the man in the pawn shop and his ma.

James Francis Callaghan was my father. He was one of eleven children, seven of whom died either at birth or in early infancy: he was the second oldest of the four who survived. Not surprisingly, his childhood impression was that 'there was always a tiny coffin under the window.' Losing children to early death was not uncommon where they lived. There was no money for doctors. One outside toilet served several families. They washed in the street at a cold water tap which froze in the winter. There was a midden in the back yard.

My father started writing about his life when he was in his eighties. Having a mistrust of computers, he wrote it on an ancient typewriter with no spellchecker, no way to change the paragraphs around and no way to delete his mistakes. It was quite laborious, and took him about five years.

He was determined that the world he had experienced and the way he saw that world would not be forgotten. His recall was accurate and vivid. He had seen through the eyes of a child, then of a young man, major events of the early twentieth century: the First World War (1914–18); the General Strike of 1926; the Great Depression in the 30s and the Second World War (1939–45). He remembers watching in awe the day in 1919 that Liverpool police went on strike (known to those who took advantage of it as 'The Loot,') and hearing the announcement of the end of the First World War being declared.

He conjures up in detail the people who lived in his neighbourhood and the jobs they did: the butcher, the baker, the chandler, the clog maker, John the cowkeeper and the woman with dropsy, Mary Ann who owned the coal yard and Big Annie who had lived through the Irish famine. He recalls details: the sounds of soldiers' boots on the cobbles, donkeys and horse-drawn carts in the street, the smell of the tanyards, the taste of raw sugar. He remembers the thrill of disappearing into the dark of the 'picture-house' ('twopence in the Balcony, penny in the Pit') and into the exciting worlds of Fatty Arbuckle, Sarah Bernhardt, Buster Keaton and Charlie Chaplin. In 1922 he listened to crackly sounds through one of the first radios.

At 14 there was just not enough money coming into the house. Like many others, despite his abilities, he had no choice but to leave school. He began work as a telegraph messenger for the London Midland and Scottish Railway company in Lime St Station, 'the vast station with its high-arched roof, the smell of burning oil, the sudden violent hiss of steam.' Every occupation, every character around him is remembered: the Inspector, 'conducting a telephonic war with signalmen,' a porter who 'bowled empty milk churns on their rims across the platform to a waiting colleague who caught and lifted them straight onto the waiting baggage car without once losing the rhythm.' Sent to work in Blackpool he collected tickets from world-famous stars – George Formby, Tom Mix, Gracie Fields and Paul Robeson. In the evenings he danced the Veleta and the Foxtrot at the Tower Ballroom, 'with Reggie Dixon on the organ' and to the music of the Big Bands (Jack Hylton, Henry Hall) at the Winter Gardens.

My father always had a fiery sense of social injustice. He knew that he was smart and hard-working and that for many young men that would certainly mean further education and a job with a 'sharp suit and bowler hat.' However, in those days, no-one in his class or in his neighbourhood stood a chance of completing school or getting more than a low-skilled job. Children around him frequently went hungry. They were beaten, suffered dire punishments for skipping school, lost limbs playing games, died of childhood diseases. He became all too aware of the chasm between the lives his family and friends lived and those of the leisured upper classes, people whose lives they only saw on the cinema screen. He writes with irony and sometimes anger about the events around him, be it the church or the police, Winston Churchill or the neighbourhood money-lender.

Candles, Carts & Carbolic is about hard lives but is also about strong, funny, resourceful people; kids without toys who invent their own games, his mother without the money to pay for a doctor whose only remedy is to walk the baby up and down the waterfront to save his life (and she does). It is about people making up satirical songs and viewing life through much Liverpool wit.

After the war there was high unemployment in Liverpool and he moved with his wife to Derbyshire, where he took university courses in the evenings and worked as a personnel officer. In the late 1950s he took his family back up north, moving to Formby, then a village. He spent his later years with my mother in Southport, Lancashire. Always at the ready to start a political discussion, he read widely and kept on top of world events. His earlier hardships and lack of education never kept him back. He remained sharp and quick-witted until his death in 2001 at the age of 91.

Jenny Callaghan,
Toronto, Canada
2011

CHAPTER ONE

Beginning School
& the End of the War

Johnny McGuire, Johnny McGuire
Yer father's gorra job
He's working in the brickfields
For four and twenty bob
An' when he comes home on Saturday night
He'll buy yer a pair o' clogs
He'll swallow a rat an' kill the cat
An' he'll marmalise the dog.

'Jesus My Lord', we sang, 'behold at length the time, when I resolve to turn away from crime.'

Eyes fix unwaveringly on the teacher as he conducts us through the weekly ritual, each one of us aware of what would befall us should we allow our minds to wander. The hymn ends, the priest takes over and we listen with mounting dread as he tells us in his thick Irish accent what we may expect should we ever deviate from the teachings of Holy Mother Church. Hell with all its pains and torments was the penalty with no hope of a reprieve from the All Powerful Being whose abode in the sky we saw quite clearly through the broken portion of a stained glass window.

Up and down the aisle the good man strides, 'Yis'll all go to Hell!' – the words spat out as he fixes some terrified child in a fanatical glare, a child that, like myself, would keep its hapless parents from sleep, screaming that the walls of the bedroom were covered in the flames of Hell. A quick glance at a nearby Station of the Cross bearing the legend 'Jesus meets His afflicted Mother' and, overcome with guilt, we came to the realisation that it was time to turn over a new leaf. We were at Sunday school. I was six years old.

School began for me at three years of age. It was 1914. Holding tightly to my mother's hand I savoured the interesting feel of the cork mat beneath my feet until the sight of a black-robed nun coming into view caused a slight panic, but after a brief conversation with my mother she gave me a friendly nod and taking my hand we entered the classroom. In the days that followed I learnt to sew a button on a square of cloth, to sing 'God Save The King' and to recite the alphabet so effectively that I was able to read a newspaper at the age of five. I suppose there were other useful lessons which I maybe forgiven for not remembering: it was a long time ago.

Memories: of my first teacher, Miss Burns, gentle, humorous, getting the other teachers to hear my version of the Marseillaise which my mother had taught me and which had them giggling hysterically. Unabashed I sang on, having been promised a ride on the rocking horse, a first-time experience not to be missed. On the make-shift stage in the school cellar where, with other infants dressed warm and white in home-made bunny costumes, I dissolve in tears on seeing my mother in the audience, who then pass me over their heads into her comforting arms. The cellar gave us shelter against Zeppelin raids when the sky where God lived became menacing and dangerous. The Catechism, price one penny, became an important part of my life. 'To whose image and likeness did God make you?' it asked. 'God made me to his own image and likeness', it replied. I took the little red book to bed with me, falling asleep reading it and in the morning my face would be stained with the dye from its covers. My sister, four years older, escorted me to school, dodging trams and wagons on the busy main road, thoughts of being accosted never entering our heads.

* * *

'The school was down by a river. Firs had been planted and the walls were covered with copper-coloured creeper. Elm trees spread their leaves and roses grew everywhere.'

Ours was early Victorian, blackened and unlovely, an architectural slag reap rising like a decaying molar from the dreary streets with their endless rows of back-to-back dwellings stretching for miles in all directions. Just short of two thousand children attended the school, divided into Infants, Juniors, Senior Boys and Girls, the latter referred to in the local patois as the Big Boys' and the Big Girls'. Classes of fifty to sixty were the norm. The most boisterous of children would be reduced to timorous silence on nearing its confines and from the day we left the haven of the Infants school to our final days as Seniors we lived in constant fear of its teachers. Moving into the Junior school we were introduced to a regime of strict discipline that never varied throughout the long, dawdling years that followed.

The main room held two classes and in the centre, her desk raised to give an all-seeing view of the children, sat Sister Margaret – woe betide the child who appeared inattentive or whispered to their neighbour or, as was often the case, fell asleep. Down would sweep the Bride of Christ to scream at the unfortunate child, followed by a couple of vicious strokes of the cane before swirling back to her throne. There was one occasion when, noticing a number of red weals on my hands, my mother grilled me until I tearfully admitted that Sister Margaret was indeed responsible, whereupon – to my utter dismay – she went to the school and confronted the 'gentle nun.' What transpired I was never to know, nor do I recollect getting any favoured treatment afterwards. Such encounters between parents and teachers were not uncommon, whilst those between fathers and male teachers often ended in fisticuffs when, strangely enough, our support was for the teacher. We sat dumb, stolid, hands clasped firmly behind our backs, speaking only in reply to the teacher, the threat of the cane ever present: punishment was swift and painful. In Standard 2b Miss Dodd, a teacher of enormous stature, ruled over a class of late starters. One of her favourite forms of punishment was to belt the legs of any child who came to school in his 'bare smackers' with a cricket stump, an unique introduction to the national game if ever there was one. In another classroom the teacher, her face contorted with anger, would pretend to tie four of the dullest children together, telling them they were a bundle of firewood.

It was in her class one winter's morning that a movement inside my boot caused me to insert an exploratory finger and flick out what I knew to be a cockroach: fortunately the incident went unobserved. Ah school days, school days, was Stonyhurst ever like that? And there was Miss Wilson coming into the classroom with a handsome sunburnt officer accompanied by Sister Margaret who said, 'Now children, who is this? Remember we spoke about him the other day,' and with one voice we yelled, 'Sir Douglas Haigh'. I wonder did Miss Wilson's handsome officer survive that monstrous war?

We must have appeared a ramshackle bunch; unwashed, dressed in hand-me-downs or in clothes picked from the smelly litter of the second-hand markets. I can remember wearing someone's cast-off knickerbockers fastened by two buttons just below the knee and a peaked cap and blouse similar to those worn by the sons of the Tsar, the effect being neither regal nor Russian.

There were barefooted children, their boots beyond repair or on loan to the pawnbroker, others bleary-eyed and hungry having got up late to a house empty of food. 'Leaving the Room' was frowned upon, allowed only in the most obviously urgent cases with the result that some smelled to high heaven. With anything from four to fourteen in a household, visits to the W.C. would have to be put off until permission was given to use the foul-smelling ones in the school-yard.

Of course we weren't all poverty-stricken: those in the front rows, offspring of artisans and shopkeepers, reasonably well-dressed but not too bright, would, despite the discrimination, have much preferred to be at the back with us, the bucks. Still, they might have missed the meaningful little smile Sister bestowed on them in passing.

On the edge of the waterfront at the north end of the city was a district which we always referred to as 'over the bridge' – to get to it it was necessary to cross over one of the canal bridges. Amongst the timber yards, coke plants, tan yards, gas works, bone stores, cattle foods, sugar houses, and any processing plant giving off a smell dwelt a tough, hell-raising and highly religious community of people. Rapid of speech, their thick Irish brogue could defy comprehension even to the Liverpool-Irish on the other side of the bridge. Morgan was a product of this little world, a fellow pupil fearing nothing and nobody. Thrashings left the teacher exhausted, Morgan unmoved. Because I lived just the other side of the bridge he regarded me as a mate, very useful, for he was a hard man to cross.

The bridges are still there and the canal, stagnant and deserted, but the community with its pubs, its church, its loyalties, the bones, the skins, the sugar, the gas and the coke plants has gone, the only remaining smell being sewage and seaweed from a desolate river.

Where are the smells of yesteryear? Singed hooves as the blacksmith fits some patient horse with its brand new shoes (7/6d for four in 1931), melting tar in the street (bursting the bubbles with our toes), horse manure, leather smelling of neatsfoot oil made from the boiled feet and shins of cattle, the sweet smell of molasses, sugar-processing at the refinery, the boiled-potato smell of oil-seed, plugs of tobacco, rum-soaked and raw, lined up on the tobacconist's counter.

The heaps of second-hand clothes in Paddy's market had their own musty smell, as did the unsold fruit dumped by the handcart women and left to rot in the back entries. To this day the sight of a burst tomato reminds me of the revolting smell.

At Flemings, where Da bought his long johns, you were met by the smell of corduroy and enormous sheets of shining brown paper. It was here that the assistant put your money in a cylinder, screwing the lid tight and sending it via a collection of tracks and pulleys to the cashier ensconced in a wire cage near the ceiling, from whence it rattled back to the assistant who tipped the contents on to the counter revealing the change and a receipt. I could have watched it for hours.

But nothing could beat the tanyards for smells. Through a knot-hole in the gate we watched men in clogs and leather aprons beating with wooden paddles at the black shiny hides that swirled round in vats of evil-looking liquid. So powerful were the smells that we held our breath until giving way to a companion demanding his turn at the knot hole. The tanyards were places to be shunned and we had no desire to work there. Handling skins was to risk anthrax which, in its final throes, according to one of our mates who heard it from his docker father, caused a man's body to arch in agony, his heels drumming frantically against his head.

* * *

Around the corner behind the tree
The Yankee sailor he waits for me
When are you going to marry me
I should like to know
For every time I look in your eye
I feel I want to go
Around the corner behind the tree ... (and so on)

There was a war on. We saw soldiers and sailors everywhere. My father joined them, a mere five feet one inch tall, blind in one eye and barely literate, called up by a country desperate to replace the slaughtered thousands and aware, though they didn't tell us until fifty years later, that there was just four weeks supply of food left in the country. It was described by the newspapers as 'Scraping the Barrel' and how right they were. His departure was memorable inasmuch as he gave me a half-penny as he left, the only thing I ever got from him in my life. The little man had hardly got into his uniform before my mother was negotiating the sale of his horse cart and coal round for twenty pounds to a shady-looking character. I watched them shaking hands on it like two men. It was the most money she had ever had or was ever likely to have.

She worked in a munitions factory, a former fruit market in Cazneau street and every Saturday morning when I went to meet her, Mr Bell the timekeeper (honest) allowed me to sit on the wooden bench below his office until the hooter sounded at twelve o'clock and crowds of women streamed out, my mother among them, in overall and funny hat, clutching her pay packet. Then, linking arms, warm and reassuring, we strolled up the street, stopping at the Post Office to collect her Allotment, which was the money my father allowed her from his shilling-a-day pay.

After the War, our mantelpiece was adorned with a massive brass shell case which she kept highly polished until, late one night, our one-room abode was disturbed by the arrival of two detectives, greatly concerned at the presence of our ornament. After earnest discussion with my mother, clearly on the defensive, the two jacks left with the souvenir, my childish mind wondering if it was live and the consequences if it had dropped from its perch.

I was seven years old when the War ended in 1918. I had learnt that our soldiers were brave beyond question and that the Germans were cowards who did terrible things to babies and nurses and who ran away at the first sight of the 'Tommies.' In school, under a picture entitled 'The Scrap of Paper', we sang 'Three Cheers For The Red White And Blue' and in the street our own version, which declared that it sticks to your belly like glue. 'The Scrap of Paper' portrayed the document in which Britain had pledged to protect Belgium from attack, causing our entry into the most awful war ever waged. At the pictures we cheered wildly as Kaiser Bill and his son Little Willie sank slowly beneath the waves, victims of the might of the British navy. We were too young to appreciate the horrors the fighting men had endured or the lesser ones they had yet to encounter, like finding work or contending with high-collared bureaucrats in order to obtain a well-earned pension. I knew about Zeppelins: I'd seen one caught in the search-lights. I knew about Ration Cards, mother's Allotment money and the sinking of the *Lusitania*. The sugar I went for, a farthings-worth wrapped in a blue paper cone, had sand in it, my father said and the meat we ate was horseflesh because the fat was bright yellow: bread had black streaks in it and eggs were so small they must be 'sarpents eggs from Egypt,' he said.

I remember the Australian soldier (I knew by his hat) who tried to kiss Susie Ellwood as they stood by the lamp post but she turned away quickly and he kissed her neck instead. I rushed in to tell my mother. Uncle Dick came to see us, bronzed and straight in his uniform with his sweetheart. Aunt Sis was a nurse at Clatterbridge Hospital and destined to be destroyed whilst still young by tuberculosis. Charlie Kershaw, a neighbour's son on leave from the Front, strode up the yard, his face beaming with pleasure, to greet my mother. The searchlights and the bullet-riddled funnel of the ferry boat, the *Iris* was displayed on the plateau of St George's Hall after the raid on Zeebrugge. The mob attacking the pork butchers at Mile End believed they were Germans, despite the photograph on the wall showing their son in British soldier's uniform. I remember my mother laying the evening paper down on her lap and saying, 'Your father's coming home. The War is over.'

Men had gone into battle; the milkman, the coalman, the post-man, the lamplighter, the docker, the bobby, the teacher, leaving behind their sad haunting songs, 'There's a Long Long Trail A winding,' 'Keep The Home Fires Burning', 'Goodbyee.'

One day in, 1919, I stood on the pavement, an interested spectator as a procession marched six abreast down Scotland Road, their medals, bowler hats and Kitchener moustaches symbols of pride and integrity. My mother said they were policemen on strike and for the next few days, as a free roaming spirit, I was witness to the consequences of the Law taking a holiday. It was a day or two before realization dawned on the local villains that there was nobody to curb their activities: the world was their oyster, at least Scotland Road was, and they wasted no time opening it.

One of the first casualties was the Mojo chewing gum factory in Bevington Bush, a stone's throw from where Seth Davis drank butter-milk all the day and whisky on a Sunday. For long afterwards, mouths bulging with chewing-gum reduced conversation to a mumble. John Hughes the grocer advertised his wares by placing open sacks of beans, sugar and tea in the window, so it was a simple matter for the mob, joined now by formerly honest and upright citizens, to smash the plate glass and drag the sacks into the street, an operation I watched with great interest. A press photograph of the incident captioned 'Caught in the Act', which I came across many years later in the reference Library, had me wondering which of the urchins in the picture was myself, but on returning for a second look I was told that the photograph had since been stolen from the library. Across the road the shattered windows of Samuels the jewellers gave way to the looters – watches, clocks, rings, lockets and chains lay among the shards of glass littering the pavement. Fights broke out, only to be quickly abandoned as the crowd turned to the real business of grabbing whatever they could lay their hands on. Standing on the fringe of all this activity I was sorely tempted, seeing some trinket lying amongst the debris of broken glass, but fear prevailed. Even a finger-lick of John Hughes' sugar would have got me a hiding from my mother. At Cranes music store the road was awash with sheet music and instruments: violins; banjos; bugles; mouth organs; Jew's harps – all made for impromptu concerts. Pianos were loaded on to handcarts; there was nobody to stop them. The army would arrive soon, but until then it was every man for himself.

Watching our own Co-operative store (Check No. 21942) being ravaged, from the first shattering of the windows to the last side of bacon being carried away, I felt sad. It was just around the corner from our house and we knew the assistants by their first names, always being careful to give the correct check number, my mother hoarding the pink slips until the divi was declared, sometimes as much as sixpence in the pound. It was so much a part of our lives and now here was this horrendous thing happening, with people jammed in the window space, fighting to get through to the shop and those inside unable to get out. A boy I knew passed me carrying an armful of brush-heads and when peace returned and I was sent on a message to the Co-op, to my eternal shame I snitched on him. I can still feel the cold stare of the assistant as she looked to see if anyone had overheard. After that the best I could hope for in the future was short weight.

When the lorries rolled up the soldiers clambered out with a clatter of hobnailed boots and rifle butts and proceeded to chase anyone in sight, beating them to the ground and, seeing this, I got frightened and ran home. The curfew that followed cleared the streets and we lay in bed hearing the soldiers running up the street clubbing the doors of the little houses with their rifle butts shouting, 'Get in your beds you bastards!' Our homes were entered without a by-your-leave and searched for items of questionable origin (the pianos?). For the poor striking policemen it was worse: they were sacked to a man and blacklisted throughout the city for jobs. By coincidence, the entire Boston police force (U.S) was on strike the same year, all 1700 of them being sacked. The Russian revolution, only two years old and still fresh in people's minds, made the authorities extremely nervous and ruthless in consequence. The policemen drafted in to replace them were Birmingham policemen my mother said. There was no Black Jack amongst them. That was the Bobby with the fierce black moustache who would collect five or six of us on each hand and, stopping the traffic left and right, take us across the main road to Orazio Fusco's where we were treated to a ha'penny ice cream pie paid for by Black Jack himself. And when the strike was over the locals, with their genius for parody, borrowed a popular wartime tune: 'How Yer Gonna Keep Em' Down On The Farm,' but they sang:

Before the War they used to wear a clog an' a boot
Now they're wearing all the fancy things from The Loot.

For those who lived through that brief lawless period it was forever referred to as 'The Loot'.

CHAPTER TWO

Food, Fun &
Fish & Chips

At school, it was now time to enter the world of the Big Boys, and with fearful stories and facial contortions the older boys left us in no doubt as to what lay in store for us at the hands of the teachers: entering the school we were decidedly nervous. Miss Linden and Miss O'Neill were part of the Big Boys establishment, taking Standards II and III in adjoining class-rooms. Our Liverpool accents were a source of amusement to them but one day Miss Linden relaxed her guard and asked us to sing one of our own songs: she must have carried the memory of what followed to her grave. Probably expecting 'Swannee' or 'Down The Road Away Went Polly', we gave her instead the song we sang during local election times when gangs of us paraded the streets singing it to the tune of 'Tramp Tramp Tramp The Boys Are Marching':

> Vote vote vote for Davy Logan
> Throw owld Johnson in the dock
> For Logan is the man
> And we'll have him if we can
> And we'll throw owld Johnson in the dock
> BY THE COCK.

No power on earth could have prevented that dramatic finale roared out decibels higher than the previous doggerel, the expression of horror on Miss Linden's face no doubt matched by that of Miss O'Neill reaching for the smelling salts.

Such things as school reports were unknown so the family were unaware of what progress I was making. My father was unconcerned but my mother encouraged me to read, passing on to me popular novels of the day, *East Lynn*, *Her Benny*, *Ishmael*, and *We Two*, by Charles Bradlaugh M.P., an atheist and a man out of his time. Most of it was way over my head but it gave me an appreciation of words which has never left me. Coming from school I took a great interest in reading the names on the century shop signs, the posters, the placards. A word on a public-house sign had me puzzled for a while: it was *Ales*, which I kept rhyming with *palace*. I got it in the end. The pay-off came later when Miss Linden earned my undying devotion by making the class sit to attention to hear me again spell the word 'vehicle'. Quinton Hogg breezing through a Classics exam couldn't have been more pleased.

In Standard IV we met our first male teacher, who got us into the right frame of mind with threats of the liberal use of the cane then, having loaded us with work, lounged in front of the fire munching on a wad of chewing-gum whilst grappling furiously with his genitals. I think he was a war casualty, at least I hope he was. None shewed such a lack of interest in his charges as this one: I doubt if he could have named half a dozen of us at the end of the year despite calling the register every day. Teachers were beings from another world, living in posh places like Anfield, Orrell Park even Hoylake. Apart from Mr Quirk, none ever mixed with us and on the rare occasions they smiled, it was not at us but at each other, a sure sign it was pay day. All of them, including the women teachers, used the cane as an aid to learning, at times six on each hand given with all the strength the teacher could muster. We tried to take it without flinching, rubbing resin on our hands believing it would lessen the pain, but it never did. 'Stand still!' you were ordered. 'Hold your hand out, straight,' – the cane would whistle down to strike neatly between thumb and forefinger, the sadists catching the tips of your fingers thereby increasing the pain. The diminutive Johnny Tart would never hold his hand out properly, his action resembling Atlas holding up the world whilst backing away crab-like from the menacing cane. Fat Godfrey invariably snatched his hand back as the cane wooshed down, the effect on the teacher being nothing short of murderous. The victims sat pale and sullen, arms folded tight, hands pressed into their armpits, the weaker ones sobbing quietly. As well as the pain it was being robbed of your dignity that really hurt, although we couldn't have explained it in those terms. In Standard V we shared our room with the slow starters of Five Vb, ruled over by an Irishman who lived in a permanent state of suppressed fury. Part-way through writing on the blackboard, he would whip round to hurl a lump of chalk at some individual, followed by the duster, covering him in chalk-dust, then reaching for the cane to vent his rage on some innocent lad already paralysed with fright.

The day the headmaster strode into the classroom, his face clearly indicating that someone was due for a pogging. I was proud of Morgan when he stood up and announced, 'It wuz me sor'. His crime: stripping the school allotment clean of every stick of rhubarb. 'I stuffed it up me gansey sor,' he said, explaining how he got it out of the school each day and then submitting to a brutal six on each hand. Much later, watching a team of powerful horses hauling a load of timber up Scotland Road, I was hailed by the driver, red-faced and laughing, flourishing his whip like some triumphant charioteer. It was Morgan. He'd found his niche and was clearly a happy man.

Meeting the headmaster years later and long retired, his abiding memory of the school was of a certain lad he had never succeeded in taming, actually quoting his name and sounding really frustrated. He hadn't the remotest idea who I was and his farewell remarks as he mounted his bicycle to the effect that I seemed to have done well suggested that it was more than he had ever hoped from his VB scally-wags. The possibility that he may have been partly responsible for their lack of achievement had obviously never occurred to him.

Our playground was littered with broken stones and tarmac and as we wore short trousers, lacerated knees were the order of the day. There was no First Aid and the only Matrons we knew were in hospitals or work-houses, so when you bled you carried on until it stopped. If anyone ever bled to death they must have kept it quiet. A mass of tarmac left behind by work-men served as a place to play King of the Castle, otherwise there were no playing facilities: we simply tore up and down in mad rushes or picked a fight. Sometimes I spoke to my sister through the railings which divided our playgrounds, feeling dreadfully sad when the whistle went and we had to part.

A corner of the rubble-strewn playground was occupied by the priest's house, a neat little mansion complete with balustrade. Steps, scrubbed and whitened, led to a massive front door and a gleaming brass door knob, in all a most impressive sight. To trespass in its hallowed precincts would, we knew, bring down the wrath of heaven, therefore to preserve its windows from damage, football was forbidden.

The most popular sport was fighting and contests started in the playground would be continued after school when a yelling mob of children would follow the combatants to the jigger between rows of tenements. Being much wider than the ordinary back entry it gave them the chance to show off their spars after the style of Jimmy Wilde or Bombardier Billy Wells before punching each other silly. I was there a few times. When Johnny Loftus was the opposition he upset me by jumping on me before we got to the jigger. I beat him.

Away from school, pain-racked fingers and demonic teachers, we lived our young lives to the full. Money was no problem: we never had any. We made our own enjoyment, like fishing for jacksharps (sticklebacks) in the pools of abandoned brickworks – lowering a potato-sack into the water then raising it, revealing a couple of struggling fish, poor things that seldom lived beyond the following day.

We played 'bang-off' using metal buttons, brass the most sought after, bone and non-metal types rejected outright. A button flattened on the tramlines and honed down to a triangle became your dimp, highly prized and never to be parted with. Holding it between thumb and forefinger with the second finger giving it impetus, you struck it hard against a wall. Your opponent then launched his dimp and if it landed within a span's length of yours he was paid a button, a span being the space bridging the two dimps by the thumb and third finger. Hours were spent playing kick-the-can. Two lines were scored in the dirt between the setts about twenty feet apart and manned by mixed teams of boys and girls, perhaps six on each side. A tin can previously flattened on the tram lines needed to be skittered towards the opposing side and if it landed on their line, they were obliged to chase the other side, who retreated running backwards. The reward on being caught was a piggyback back to the starting line. Shrieks of laughter and wonderful fun.

Cherry stones were cherrywobs to us. An equal number from each player placed at the base of a downspout would require each contestant in turn to flick a cherrywob up the spout and any of the stones struck by the emerging missile could then be claimed by that player. Probably the only one of our games where 'rain stopped play.' What did we call it? 'Up the spout', of course. Another was to knock as many stones as possible out of a chalked circle using your own favourite cherrystone, an unusually large one, disputes arising when a stone was found to be weighted with a sizeable portion of lead.

Ollies, marbles if you want to be posh, meant three holes about six feet apart dug in the gutter, the object being to traverse the holes whilst keeping your opponent from achieving the same by some well-directed aims at his ollie. Throwing was considered sissy and although the ollies were enormous we used a very professional flick. To negotiate from the first hole to the third and back was known as 'up for lasses', the final stretch as 'up for segs'. It was a popular game played by the grown ups for as much as fourpence a game and watched by great crowds on the 'oller.' Some time in the past a caring adult had chiselled into the paving flags the names of far-away places: Egypt, Japan, America, India and such and the young ones not yet ready for the boisterous games of the older children would form up as trains chugging along the gutter giving passable imitations of train whistles. Imagine the frustration to be called in for bed just as the train was approaching your stop, New Zealand.

It was the practice in our infant days to dress the boys in girls' clothes even up to the age of five, useful in a family where there was an abundance of girls (next door to us had five). Dress for the older boys was short pants, a union shirt (collarless) long stockings, boots and a gansey. Shoes were a rarity and considered cissy. Underpants were yet to come and handkerchiefs were as absent as they are today, the sleeves of the gansey utilised for this purpose, eventually taking on the sheen of fish scales. Trousers wore out, inevitably at the seat, the protruding shirt tail giving a clear indication of one's social standing. Long trousers weren't worn until fifteen or sixteen and how well I remember when my turn came, by which time I had been working for two years. I stood at our wicket gate, one 'longy' shewing tentatively to the outside world for some time before venturing into the street and the world of adults. Children and parents stared in genuine admiration. You can't begin to understand the thrill of that day: it was Graduation Day, Bar Mitzvah, Manhood.

Because of the tradition of dressing boys in girls clothing, the sight of Nippy's red flannel drawers, he of the five sisters, when we went fishing, aroused little comment. Fishing meant lying full length over a shop grid and with a piece of wire and a bent spoon attempting to hook anything of value from the mass of debris below. Skill, patience, concentration and the encouragement of a horde of kids were essential to bring the loot to the surface, which often fell back just as it was within your grasp. Prime targets were farthings, halfpennies, pennies, threepenny-bits and sixpences, otherwise known as fudges, megs, wonners, joeys and tanners. Bobs (shillings) were rare; the loser would have pulled the grid and the shop apart to retrieve it. Sometimes we tried the sewer grids, one in each gutter, but we were invariably put off at the sight of dead water rats floating belly up.

Hopscotch, jacks and ollies and a gentle form of skipping rope was strictly for the girls accompanied by age old ditties, 'Manchester Races Buttermilk Cream' or 'Call in my very best Friend,' and one recalling an historic event of long ago:

> Queenie Queenie Caroline
> Dipped her hair in turpentine
> Turpentine made it shine
> Queenie Queenie Caroline.

But of all the games we played none gave us more fun than skipping rope, a much wilder affair than that played by the girls, when all the boys and girls joined in, the rope an inch thick, smacking the setts in menacing fashion as it was turned by a couple of buxom housewives. There was no room for milkmaid cavorting: it took nerve, preceded by a couple of half-hearted attempts to dart in and start skipping. The girls were expert, but the boys often joined in, heads bent, fearful of being knocked flat as faster and faster the rope turned until a final frenzied burst of speed to the chant of 'pitch, patch, pepper' brought the wild dance to a close. Crimson with their efforts the housewives relaxed, peals of laughter from the children, relieved to have come through unscathed, then a brief spell before being joined by the young men and women drawn from their houses by the merriment. Such simple glorious fun.

On summer evenings the streets swarmed with children engaged in some form of activity. There were no wallflowers: it was time for play and play they did. Occasionally the games were interrupted by the ladies from Lee Jones's handing out tickets for a free meal and a game of ping-pong but we always refused: to accept charity was to risk a hiding from our mothers.

Except during the summer holidays, bed at seven o'clock was strictly enforced, at which hour the air resounded with the cries of mothers to their offspring to come in for bed. There was never any argument and Mary, Tommy, Jimmy, Kathleen, Eddie and Theresa all obeyed the call. There were no Waynes, Mary-Lous or Billy-Joes. We took our names from the saints – who better? Then a wash in front of the fire and the usual scuffle with the face cloth in the hands of Ma, a final admonition not to forget your prayers then off to bed to lie and watch the shadows cast by the candle making the walls come alive.

From the darkness pressing against the window come the night sounds, the sergeant's stick striking the paving flags calling the patrolling bobby to their planned rendezvous, the forlorn cry of a newspaper lad, the last of his papers still unsold, the clang of hammer on steel as the repairmen work on the tram tracks, their voices made clear by the stillness of the night. Saturday night had its own sounds, the sad distant song of a lone reveller homeward bound, the women coming from the alehouses standing in the gutter to relieve themselves in tumultuous splashes.

An unfailing duty for children was to 'go messages', and after school they thronged the shops. My favourite was the Maypole, where an assistant armed with two wooden paddles gouged a lump out of a barrel-shaped edifice of butter on the counter then slapped, patted and coaxed it into a neat rectangle before wrapping it in crisp white paper. The floor of the shop was sprinkled liberally with sawdust and everything about it, counter, shelves and assistants was scrupulously clean. Grocers' shops were plentiful, selling bacon, lard, butter, cheese and eggs straight off the Irish Boat: a quarter of bacon for threepence; eggs two for three ha'pence; half a pound of cheese for fourpence; corned beef; delicious brawn and more often than not, change out of a shilling.

At the butchers massive carcasses hung from the ceiling; ankle-deep in sawdust we watched an assistant carve generous lumps out of the bloodied meat destined for the plates of the menfolk. I'd like to have seen their expressions faced with a salad.

Food was bought in every day, the highlight being the visit to the pork butchers late on Saturday night where, because there was no refrigeration, pigs' heads, hams and tasty pieces of offal were practically given away. Whole sheets of ribs could be had for sixpence, picking your own from the barrel, served with boiled cabbage, dry bread and a bottle of Guinness, price sevenpence for the parents. It was indeed a feast for the gods.

Smells of chlorine, bleach, carbolic, candles and paraffin met you at the Chandlers. There was red raddle for window sills, sandstone for the front step, the really house-proud housewife scrubbing the front of her little house down to the gutter. We bought gas mantles, dipping the fragile mesh into vinegar which made them burn brighter and last longer. Snuff in all shades and strengths was sold and when some old biddy sent me for twopenn'th of Fine Irish, I watched for Mrs Parkinson the chandler to spill some but she never did.

Mr Skillicorn was our baker, short, fat, bald and covered in flour dust. I spotted him once in a crowded Brueghel painting and I said to myself that's our Mr Skillicorn. Nobody today could ever make bread like Mr Skillicorn, or barmcakes soft as marshmallows, delicious enough to eat without butter. Mrs Skillicorn, herself dusted with flour, took your order, 'tin or oven bottom', and you waited on the wooden boards of the shop floor until a perspiring baker emerged from the back with trays of heavenly-smelling, brown-crusted loaves, each one weighed carefully and should it prove to be below the two pounds required by law then a slice from a spare loaf was added. The 'jockey on a loaf', we called it. On the way home it was impossible to resist picking pieces from the warm crusty loaf in its tissue-paper wrapping tucked under your arm – well worth the clip over the ear your mother gave you when she saw the damage.

Behind the counter at the Chemist's were rows of wooden drawers, labelled in abbreviated Latin, containing substances of mysterious origin. I can't ever remember seeing the chemist open one. Perhaps they were just for show, like the enormous apothecary jars with their red and green liquids. Very real though were the sinister black leeches floating up and down in their jars.

Beechams Pills, four a penny, came wrapped in a twist of paper, medicines with exotic names like Syrup of Figs, Paregoric, Ipehachuana Wine, and a not-so-exotic thick white emulsion, horrible to look at and even more horrible to swallow. Many of the panaceas and palliatives were opium-based: not that our parents knew but they put the baby to sleep which was all that mattered. In great demand was the 'Grip-Tight Pacifier' – rammed into the mouth of a yelling infant it saved many a harassed mother from going mad. If the chemist was in a good mood he might present you with an Oracle, a square of white paper which, when touched off at a certain spot by a lit cigarette-end, produced a spark which followed an invisible line of saltpetre forming the head of a famous person, popular ones being Lord Carson and Lloyd George

Our tobacconist was a fussy little man who got exasperated if we were slow to name our requirements so we usually took our time. I was sent regularly for half an ounce of thick twist, price fourpence, for my father who smoked it and the same for John the Cowman who chewed it. Needless to say I sneaked a taste of it and only by a great effort avoided being sick. The tobacconist had an enormous son always ready for a fight. He wore the first pair of brogues I ever saw.

Swarthy and sad-looking Orazio Fusco stood on a wooden crate, attired in off-white jacket and apron, dispensing the finest ice cream in the world, ice cream bulging from all sides of the sandwich, price one penny. For a half-penny he would fill a cornet or a pie to overflowing, accompanied with elaborate flourishes of the spatula. We never heard him speak or saw him smile, perhaps longing for the warmth of his homeland.

At Ellis's the linoleum shop we bought oilcloth for the table and at Moss's the gents outfitters, caps, best quality, one and eleven three-farthings. Appletons were the Clog makers: most of their customers were the bargees from off the Leeds and Liverpool canal, squat, weather-beaten fellows wearing corduroys which covered enormous posteriors. The story goes that a bevy of these canal-dwellers monopolised the bar in a pub in such a way that the locals couldn't get near, whereupon one of the locals went away and returned with a sackful of rats, which he emptied on to the bar.

* * *

Everything required for our daily needs could be had within a few minutes walk of our homes: post-office; pawnshop; chandler; iron-monger; milliner; tailor; coalyard; barber shop – a penny for a haircut and a humbug to suck on your way home. If you decided not to be scalped, the barber placed a tin basin on your head and sheared round the rim. There were cinemas – seven within walking distance – music halls, theatres, pubs a-plenty, churches galore, second-hand furniture stores, second-hand clothes shops, tattoo parlours and a Penny Bazaar. From the Salt Man, his saw rasping through the blocks on his handcart, we bought rock salt, a foot square and an inch thick for twopence. In the evening, bent under the weight of the cradle of window panes, came the old man, heralding his arrival with a mournful cry of 'Windows!'

At Dr Coughlan's surgery we sat on wooden benches, moving round clockwise, alert for the tinkle of the bell announcing the end of one consultation and the beginning of the next. Despite the doctor's best efforts, the undertakers were never short of work; funerals were an everyday sight.

Bright lights, mouth-watering smells and the hiss of sizzling fat meant the chip shop and the queue of customers moving dutifully towards the counter, the anticipation of the joys ahead giving them a trance-like appearance. Sixpence bought a batter-encrusted fish and enough chips to fill a sheet of newspaper. Then home through the darkened streets, feeling the vinegar and the grease starting to seep through the layers of newspaper, the delight on the faces of the family as the wrapper is opened to reveal the feast. Reinforced with bread, margarine and further lashings of salt and vinegar, it fed the **family**.

Once, finding my fish and chips wrapped in pages of the *London Illustrated News*, all of eight years old, I read of the sinking of the *Titanic*. The dramatic drawings of the great ship plunging to its end and the name of Captain Edward John Smith were imprinted on my mind for ever.

Teatime was the highlight of the day, when the breadwinner took his place at the table seated in *his* chair, the evening paper alongside his plate and not to be touched until he had read it from end to end. Ma cut the bread, buttering each piece before handing it round. There was no helping yourself: you sat mute, took whatever was given to you and ate it. If you didn't, it was assumed you were sick, which meant a Beechams pill or worse. Soup made from a cod's head might be on the menu – 'Ask him to cut it as near the tail as possible'. It wasn't popular, not like rabbit, which came in shiploads from Australia, packed tight in wooden crates, bits of white fur sticking through the slats like symbols of surrender. They cost ninepence skinned. 'Can yer mother skin a rabbit?' we sang. My grandchildren were disgusted when I told them how much I had enjoyed a rabbit's head, but then they've never known real hunger.

> Oh, the pie was placed upon the table
> an' we all made a rush for the door
> Me ol' man fainted on the floor
> an' I went through the door with a bish bang
> The cat started laughing and the dog fell dead
> The monkey up the chimney did a guy
> As long as I live I never will forget
> The day we ate the rabbit pie.

That's what happens when the family eats something which so much resembles a cat.

Friday night was special. We had bacon and egg for tea, of which I was particularly fond, and marmalade specially for my father. There was no gas or electricity in the house and all the cooking was done on the fire of a Zebo-blackened range of the sort the Heritage crowd go all sentimental over these days. They should have seen my mother struggling with it: pouring water through the opening in the top of the hob to clear the accumulated soot, then working the damper in and out to divert it into the ashpit, her arms singed by the fire built up to heat the oven, her face a mask of sweat. Quite often her efforts came to nothing when the chimney decided to dislodge its load of soot, thereby 'drowning' the fire and putting an end to all thoughts of cookery. If it was Sunday I would be rushed off with the dinner to the baker in Latimer street who, for a fee of fourpence, specialised in cooking Sunday dinner for those unable or unwilling to perform this most sacred of functions. It tasted delicious, as did our own when the oven was in the mood, the chimney in good humour and the bottom didn't fall out of the grate.

Sunday, dear remembered Sunday, the boys scrubbed clean, the girls with their lovely high complexions, clothes neatly pressed after the ritual of Saturday night with the tin bath in front of the fire, shrieks of nervous laughter as a kettle of hot water is added to the bath – cries of 'Ma, he's looking!' as a curious sibling ventures too close. To church, where it is standing room only at every Mass, the fresh young voices of the choir, the swell of the music as the organist gets into his stride, the prayers, the incense, the opulent vestments of the priests, proof indeed of the awesome power of the Church. Then home, feeling pious and famished, the Church in its wisdom forbidding you to eat before taking Holy Communion. Salt fish and bacon for breakfast (maybe pineapple chunks for tea?) and throughout, the certain knowledge that this was a holy day and you were, at least for the time being, free from sin.

After breakfast and after the priest had collected the weekly tribute, Da settles down to his newspaper, *The Empire*, the *News of The World* or *The Chronicle*, all priced twopence and delivered by lads whose arms must have ached, for the papers were enormous, giving them added value as their penultimate fate was to be torn into squares and hung in the lavatory. The contribution they made to a child's ability to read was considerable: they certainly helped me. Nearing two o'clock I'd be sent to the pub for two pints of mild beer, clutching our white quart jug and sixpence, hearing the noisy gossip and the raucous laughter of the men in their high-crowned bowler hats and collarless shirts, the air thick with the fug from clay pipes and the sour smell of beer, and in the Snug the heavy-breasted, wide-bottomed women debating whose lad I was. Pausing only to take a sip, I hurry home to join in the ritual of Sunday dinner, when the door is locked to all callers and strict silence reigns at the table. Dinner over, Da resumes his study of the newspaper before retiring to bed to 'rest with Mother', bringing joy to the Vatican and the warmongers and dismay to the upper classes – 'My dear, they breed like rabbits'. For our parents, Sunday was simply a brief interruption from work. Beyond the privilege of working they asked for nothing and they got nothing.

When the last customers had left the pubs the quiet of Sunday descended like a pall. Cinemas, factories, mills and shops were silent, trams were few, cars a rarity. It was the day to visit the sick (one hour only, strictly enforced by a no-nonsense Matron), or flowers and a prayer at the cemetery. The tiny ones visited Grandma for their Sunday penny, the older ones went to the park to play hide and seek or to climb trees, all the while keeping a sharp lookout for the Parkies ever ready to use their sticks. They may have headed for the Museum in the town, where the big attraction was the seal, which spent its life amongst the rows of Egyptian mummies and assorted sarcophagi, swimming aimlessly hour after hour in a tank not much larger than itself, head forever poised enquiringly above the water as if searching for the rescuer that never would arrive. Its good to know that such cruelty would not be tolerated today.

Across the road on St Georges Plateau we joined in the noisy but cheerful music provided by the Sally Army, although we knew they were some sort of Proddy Dogs, singing 'We Shall Meet beyond the River where the surf ceases to foam' (or 'We Shall have Meat and also Liver' – my mother's version) before heading for The Lanny to see the Liners, stopping awhile to gaze at the machine on Water Street that claimed to be the nearest thing to perpetual motion. If you were flush, the ferry to Seacombe cost a penny, from where you walked to New Brighton, which was more upmarket; if you were really well off then it could be the paddle steamer to Eastham, which cost fourpence

Back in Scotland Road down certain back entries heavily guarded by look-out men (dowseys) games of Pitch and Toss, Crown and Anchor and heavy card games flourished, adult pastimes and of no interest to us.

One shop of fond memory stayed open, Spencer's the Spruce shop. It sold soft drinks, stick-a-lice – a straw-coloured twig which frayed in your mouth when chewed, exuding a sap sweeter than sugar – and liquorice sticks as thick as a broom handle. After we had got past the Sunday school stage and began to take an interest in girls we would sit in the semi-darkness of the shop, its row of pumps a daring suggestion of a real pub sipping a glass of Vimto, one penny, trying to think of something to say. I've gone there with a pretty twelve year-old, ordered two Vimtos, 'hot please', and sat for half an hour having said less than a dozen words. Such wondrous childish innocence, never to be recaptured.

Football was strictly cloth cap. To play it in the street was to risk being arrested, so we walked for miles to some derelict wasteland away from shops and houses, playing ourselves to a standstill with the final score thirty one to twenty nine, or some such score, then trudged home.

There was one memorable Sunday when, after church, we met in the street to pick the teams. Amidst the arguing and general milling about, ten year-old Paddy Doyle sat on the pavement, feet in the gutter, flicking a coin in the air, catching it neatly and studying it for heads or tails. This was Paddy's favourite pastime long before George Raft thought of it, and possibly the cause of the trouble which followed.

Without warning I was crushed against the wall by a huge man who told me I was under arrest for gambling. I was shocked. Most of the rest had fled but Paddy stayed around to check what was going on and would later recount with mischievous glee how my knees were trembling, and how right he was, for to be arrested those days was a serious matter. There were four of these hulks, the other three having captured two brothers ages thirteen and ten. My mother was naturally upset, my father uninterested. Ten year-old Henry was too young for the Magistrates court so all three of us had to appear at the Juvenile court at 10 am on the following day.

At the court we were met by a most affable detective (one of the Crime Squad) evidently anxious to put us at our ease, which meant plead guilty and hope for the mercy of the court. Unfortunately for his plans, he failed to notice my mother, who gave him one of her famous looks of contempt before he herded us into court.

Each detective took the oath and each described how the raid was organised. The four had separated and whilst two split up and went up adjoining streets meeting at the top of ours, the other two came from the bottom end and so the trap was set. They then described how they had seen us handling coins in the process of playing Pitch and Toss, an illegal gambling game. I simply couldn't believe my ears: we were in deep trouble.

Thirteen year-old Joey was questioned first and declared firmly that we were not playing Pitch and Toss but he was very nervous and it came out Totch and Piss, so that in spite of our serious position Henry and I were desperately trying to stifle our giggles. When it came his turn Henry was too far gone to speak, so the magistrate, Stuart Deacon, ordered me to explain.

My mother had instructed me to speak up clearly and to tell the truth and I did both. The magistrate then asked some people seated at a large oval table behind us if they had any questions and one said he would like me to repeat my evidence which I did, word for word. The case was dismissed.

Although this took place many many years ago I still feel a twinge of anger thinking of those men, married no doubt and with children of their own, deliberately setting out to ruin a child's life, parading us like criminals. What impelled them to act as they did, fear of their superiors, a desire for promotion or contempt for the people of Scotland Road I don't know, but I have reason to believe it was the latter. These were not the friendly bobbies of fiction but plain clothes detectives prowling the streets, looking for the slightest infringement of the law and failing that, pouncing on a bunch of harmless children.

CHAPTER THREE

Treacle, Gumboils & Fleas

Scotland Road was an exciting place for a lad with its noise, bustle and movement. The pavements were thronged, very tall policemen strolled in twos, Lascar sailors (Johnnies) padded along in single file, heads adorned with three or four decrepit looking top hats acquired after much haggling from Paddy's market; sailors – there were always sailors noisy and tipsy showing off their Western Ocean roll to impress the judys; women, their heads hidden under Paisley shawls, hurried to the shops to get something in for ' 'is tea', or to the washhouse for a well-earned gossip, lashings of hot water and carbolic soap for the washing in the baskets they carried on their heads.

Powerful draught horses hauled wagons laden with the produce of the world, raw sugar for the refineries, hides for the tanyards, tobacco, timber, grain, oil and fruit. Steam wagons belching smoke sped along at a steady ten miles an hour, the two-man crew feeding the boiler and studying the dials like real engine drivers. Donkey carts dodged in and out of the maelstrom of traffic, the hardy mokes setting up a mournful braying when brought to a standstill. Soldiers marched to the barracks at Seaforth and others marched away to embark at the Landing Stage for some foreign field and bloody conflict.

From the newspaper offices high-stepping ponies pulling two-wheeled traps galloped up the road, the drivers re-enacting their own version of Ben Hur. At points along the way bundles of newspapers were hurled on to the pavement, where the waiting Exy-coshers pounced on them to cut the string, share them out and tear off in all directions, selling them as quickly as possible and getting back for the next delivery. Ninepence a dozen the newsboys paid for them, thirteen to the dozen, underfed, boots often in tatters, soaked to the skin coughing their lungs up and all for a profit of fourpence a dozen.

And the trams, there was always one in sight apart from Sunday, clean, cheap, reliable, the drivers in the open cabs facing torrential rain, blizzards and the all-pervading fog – all without exception sporting a King George V beard and moustache. It was possible then to travel all the way to Manchester by tram.

Skipping 'leckies was exciting but risky. Pick one where the conductor was on the top deck collecting fares then skip on with a balletic flourish holding tight to the handrail, one leg dangling nonchalantly in the air and conscious of the admiring stares of the urchins on the parapet, then, just as the conductor returns red-faced and swearing, drop off casually, giving him a insolent, parting stare. Riding at the rear of the tram, gripping the big brass lamp, stomach pressed to the fender and straining to lift your toes clear of the setts was also exciting but uncomfortable. As the tram gathered speed there came a point of no return and the realisation that if you let go your chin would meet the fender with awesome results, not to mention the effect on your knee-caps. It was then that the conductor, becoming aware of a stowaway, leaned over and belaboured you with his cap until the tram slowed and you were able to stand up and exchange personal comments with your grinning tormentor.

When the treacle wagon trundled by we rolled a sleeve up, ducked between the wheels and scooped out an armful of the delicious black stuff from the discharge pipe where the remains of its viscid cargo continued to drip. It was a dangerous pastime and the driver, used to the reckless games of the kids could hardly be blamed when one of the iron-shod wheels made ten year-old Alec one-legged for the rest of his life.

We rode on the axles of hansom cabs and funeral coaches until someone shouted 'whip behind' and the coachman, checking our reflection in the shop windows, sent his whip curling delicately to the rear by which time we were safe on the parapet from where Mad Munro might get our attention. Flat-capped, sunburnt and wizened he played a barrel-organ decorated with pictures of the Battle of Jutland, at which place we assumed he had lost his legs, for Mad Munro's truncated body spent its days on a home-made four-wheeled platform barely six inches from the ground. Knowing there was no hope of a contribution from us he would chase us on his makeshift carriage as we ran away yelling and laughing at the absurdity of it. At the warehouses, where wagons waited to be unloaded, we slit the sacks just enough to gouge out handfuls of black unrefined sugar called Togee and the same with the sacks of locusts, dried wrinkled beans, incredibly sweet.

We stop to gaze in admiration at the two young men in their five dollar steel-grey suits and American trilbys bought in New York, greeting each other with loud exclamations shaking hands like long-lost friends though chances were they only lived two streets from each other. Having made the one trip on a liner, one week out, one in port and one week home they had even acquired a Western Ocean roll. The real Merchant Navy men, away for anything up to two years, regarded them with contempt, calling them 'first trippers'.

Then with no more than a glance at the huddle of rags in the shop doorway, a meths drinker, betrayed by the green tinge on a face lost and hopeless, we hurry on to Cissie Bristows, hoping for any faded apples too far gone to be saleable. Big, bouncy rosy-cheeked Cissie, always cheerful in spite of her husband having been one of the thousands who never came back from what some lame-brained writer has called the Great Adventure, she rarely failed us, and the 'fades' went down to join the Togee, the locusts and the treacle.

Whoever had named the streets which were our playground had highly-developed classical tastes. We played under the banners of Ben Johnson, Alexander Pope (in full), Addison, Gay, Dryden, Milton, Chaucer, Juvenal, Virgil; if these illustrious names had any effect on the inhabitants of the dark, dank streets thus honoured it didn't show.

Defying wind and rain, the acetylene flares wheezed and whiffled, reaching out into the night then suddenly drawing back to light up the faces of the hucksters shouting the merits of their wares to an audience enjoying the excitement of Saturday night on the 'Oller.

The Lino man emphasised his last and final offer by giving the roll of linoleum a resounding slap, and when the Crockery man failed to tempt the crowd with his spiel he pretended annoyance by hurling the rejected items at the wall behind him, a shocking waste we thought as we crept behind the wagon, hoping to retrieve an unbroken cup or plate.

The black man sold tins of toothpowder (it was precipitated chalk), giving his audience a spellbinding account of life in the African jungle, telling how the natives searched for a particular herb to cure some form of sickness. This required staring into the sky for a sign: it was also the signal for me to leap on his back as he careered around the circle of spectators in imitation of an indian woman and her child, myself praying that I wouldn't fall off. My reward was twopence, wealth indeed. I never learnt what all this had to do with toothpowder – we used soot straight from the chimney.

Under a huge poster of a Regency dandy, 'Johnny Walker Whisky 1820–1920 Still Going Strong', the local Strong Man challenged anyone to tie him up, any way they liked, declaring he would free himself in five minutes. There was much nudging and whispering, 'He'll never get out of that lot, the feller that tied him up ties the papers for the Echo.' He never failed but by the time he went round with the hat most of his audience had drifted away.

Amongst the various begging bowls hosted by the Church were the Foreign Missionary Society, the Good Shepherd Fund and Peter's Pence, which I suppose was the Pope's pocket money. As well as the glow brought on by the benevolent smile of the teacher, the children who contributed most to the Good Shepherd fund were invited to a 'do' at the Archbishop's residence way out in the country, a sort of ecclesiastical garden party and to see those kids coming in on Monday morning looking so smug and sanctimonious was hard to bear. Needless to say I never qualified for the honour. Was I envious? Of course I was.

The other members of the class bathing in the sunshine of the teacher's smile were the would-be priests, handsome usually, golden-haired always, facing twelve years of intensive indoctrination, five years more than demanded by the Jesuits. For the rest of us it was regular thrashings and the stifling of any signs of talent.

* * *

Arriving at Standard VI we met a teacher who appeared to have a genuine interest in us. Terence Quirk was teacher, choir master and football team manager, and he even joined us in the playground, something the other teachers wouldn't dream of doing. He arranged political debates and on one occasion tried to teach us the basics of Logic: we were baffled. It was Liberal and Conservative those days, with a highly vocal Irish Nationalist party (our M.P., T. P. O'Connor, being one of its leaders) and the Labour party beginning to make itself heard. Each class spent half an hour every morning in prayer and religious instruction and I was picked to read to the class a passage from the New Testament, by which Quirky hoped to enlighten us regarding the beauty of the English language.

As the Scouse accent was then even more unintelligible than it is today, he faced a monumental task. Incidentally, the term Scouse referred to a recipe born out of poverty and the cheapest cuts of meat. Applied to an individual it meant that person was the lowest of the low, a remark often leading to bloodshed.

From this man, years ahead of his time, we heard about Shakespeare, Francis Bacon, Hillaire Belloc, G. K. Chesterton, John Mansfield, Rupert Brooke, Byron and that ultra-jingoist Henry Newbolt. 'There's a breathless hush in the Close tonight', 'If I should die think only this of me', and my own favourite, 'Quinquereme of Ninevah from distant Ophir. Rowing home to haven in sunny Palestine!'. Was there ever such a lovely poem for someone who treasured words?

In between theses intellectual pursuits, Quirky, like the others, had his moments and when he started towards you, the cane swishing angrily in his left hand, the desire to hide under the desk was overwhelming. I was no blue-eye and more than once felt his wrathm though I might have been forgiven for allowing my attention to wander through watching the fleas playing hide and seek in the head of the boy in front. The wonder was that he never scratched himself.

Failure to attend school meant a visit from the school-board, Mr Percival (Mr Be Merciful) and only the imminence of death was accepted as an excuse. Persistent truancy, 'sagging', could mean the offender being sent to one of the dreaded Industrial schools, ready-made recruitment centres for the armed forces where one type of brutality was exchanged for one even harsher. The stories that filtered through of the regime in these schools evoked fears among us akin to those of criminals faced with the prospect of Devil's Island.

Ten year-old Danny Woods was sent to an Industrial School some-where in the country for persistent truancy, only to meet his death on the live rail of the local suburban line trying to escape. How the child must have sobbed crossing the dark mysterious fields, behind him the grim barracks, ahead of him not a shred of hope of comfort from parent, teacher or priest. The deserted streets and the blank silent houses offered little joy when you were absent from school, whilst the dread prospect of facing the teacher on the morrow weighed heavily. The real truants wandered the streets begging bread from the dockers, in constant fear of the police, or worse still of meeting Mr Percival.

I was accepted for the choir and I loved it; the music, the whispered instructions, the thrill of a full throated crescendo, the feet of the organist dancing on the wooden slats. The choirmaster draped sheets of heavy black paper over an easel, wetting the sheets so that the chalked words he wrote on them stood out stark white, like magic. We sang in English, Latin and Greek (Kyrie Eleison, Greek for 'Lord Have Mercy'), and for all I know many other languages, without the vaguest idea of what the words meant. There was never any explanation. Life was like that: nobody took you to one side to say, ' Look son, this is the way its done', which is why to this day I blame the choir master (Quirky) when he sent two of his newest recruits to pump the organ. In the cramped dusty confines of the organ loft we pumped vigorously until the lead on its string reached the 'full' mark. Then we hastened back to join in the singing, only to hear the organ expire in the middle of a rousing Domine salvum fac.

Keen though I was, it became clear that I would never become one of the stars and when one of these failed to turn up, it was usually me who was sent to round him up. One boy with a wonderful voice and a father, mother and older brothers all alcoholics, was often absent from Benediction on Sunday evening and when I arrived to coax him back to the fold it was to find the tiny terrace house in a drunken turmoil and the lad in tears. It was a relief to me, and to the choir master, when I returned with the sweet singer in tow.

We performed at eleven o'clock Mass, at Benediction on Sundays and Thursdays, and at the all-too-frequent Requiem Mass for the Dead where we sang the Stabat Mater, surely the most doleful hymn in the history of church music.

> Stabat Mater Dolorosa
> Juxta Crucem Lachrymosa
> Dum Pendebat Filius.

> At the Cross, Her station keeping
> Stood the mournful Mother weeping,
> Close to Jesus to the last.

It was a relief when the service ended. What with the coffin draped in its purple and black pall, the dolorous hymn and the gloom of the church, it was no place for a healthy ten year-old.

Once a year a band of Friars descended on the parish, preaching for six weeks to packed houses, the object being to winkle out back-sliders and heretics and also to bolster the faithful. The theme song of the mission was 'Alleluia', which we sang endlessly: it seemed to have no other words. My mother said it meant 'Sally I hardly knew yer,' a comment on some black-sheep returning to the fold. She could be irreverent at times.

There were four priests in our church, one a Canon, all well-fed, well-shod and in complete control of the spiritual lives of their parishioners, all eight thousand of them. They shared the Masses on Sundays at seven, eight, nine, ten and eleven o'clock, Benediction on Sunday and Thursday evenings and the daily Masses of which there were three (some people went to Mass every day of their lives). There was also the morbid Requiem Mass and of course Sunday school, usually taken by the Wild Irish Boy. In between all this activity they married people – marriage being quite popular those days – and confirmed the children.

After the last Mass on Sunday the priests visited the homes of the faithful to collect alms, accompanied by an alter boy in civvies, who ran on ahead alerting the householder by banging on the door and shouting 'Priest!', thereby giving the woman of the house time to rake through her purse. The minimum was a penny, twopence acceptable, threepence brought a glow to the Father's face and an enquiry as to your well-being.

Our Canon was the daddy of them all when it came to extracting money from his parishioners. Squat, foghorn-voiced and copper-faced with good living he would enter a pub and demand twopence from every customer and get it. If there was no one at home he didn't hesitate to take an appropriate amount from the purse on the mantelpiece: anywhere, any time, he never failed to put the fear of God into man, woman or child.

Pride and fear ensured the success of the Collection and few failed to contribute; after further donations at Mass and Benediction some women would be down to their last penny and contemplating a 'bundle for the pawnshop'. Father Parker, very English, regarded us with disdain, once informing the congregation that he didn't depend on it for a living. I can see him now, florid-faced, heavy-jowled, gazing down from the pulpit at the shawl-clad crones below him, their piteous pleas to the Creator to forgive them their trespasses leaving him unmoved.

The influence they exercised on their flock was considerable and many a fighting-mad parishioner defying family, neighbours and police could be brought to heel by the mere threat of sending for the priest. The message they preached was that if you endured the poverty and degradation of this world without complaint, your reward would come in the next, allowing for a few thousand years in Purgatory as a preliminary.

There were times, few in number, when we might escape the wrath of parents and teachers. The priest was different: behind him was his Boss, from whom there was no escape. The ultimate crime, earning a mortal sin, was to miss Mass, so every Monday morning a priest came to the school to sort out the malingerers.

How virtuous we felt as the Mass-missers stood up, sweating with fear and shame, amongst them a lad beaten many times until it was discovered his parents were of different creeds and to please one meant deceiving the other. Those who had missed Mass and were afraid to own up carried the double burden of one transgression and the unspoken lie to the priest and we were only too well aware that if you died in your sleep in that state you went straight to Hell.

The poverty in the surrounding streets could hardly have gone unnoticed by the clergy when making their rounds, such as the children wearing 'police clothes', a common enough sight and a cruel indignity inflicted on deprived children. These symbols of poverty were made of a corduroy so hard and rigid that the jacket could stand up alone without collapsing. Designed without collars (the Eton influence here), the child's neck would become raw with the constant chafing, the short trousers having a similar effect on the backs of the knees. Iron shod clogs and black knee length stockings completed the appalling outfit.

The girls dress, a heavy drab serge patterned on Quaker lines, was obviously intended to outlive its wearer, also burdened with clogs, black stockings and God knows what underneath, clothes that were the brainchild of some middle-class sadist who believed that if you were poor it was your own fault, worn by children despised even by those who themselves existed from one day to the next. Tommy Fisher was condemned to wear such clothes. A couple of inches shorter than me and an aggressive little lad, he enjoyed bullying me until I plucked up enough courage to fight him: hampered by his police clothes and his height, the result was inevitable. Feeling sorry for him, I took him to our house after school where he amused himself picking worms from our thin strip of garden and putting them through the mangle. Thus are friendships formed.

Where Tommy lived, whole families existed in foul, damp cellars sharing a single lavatory with other families occupying the same house, streets filthy and badly-lit standing row upon dreary row on a hillside from where, during his ill-fated invasion, Prince Rupert had once surveyed the town below.

Times and places have changed but that was the way things were those days. In later years I learnt that the owner of these hovels was the Marquess of Salisbury, High Church and head of the Cecil family. Possibly about the time Tommy and his sister were collecting their police clothes from the police station, young David Cecil was spending his holidays between the family homes of Hatfield and Cranborne. Years later, I heard him speak on television in an accent that, if she heard it, must have decided the Queen to improve on hers. I wonder if when he died was he called upon by his God to explain the awful existence of Tommy and the thousands like him.

Disease was never far away, diphtheria and the fever van, bronchitis and galloping consumption made gaps in our circle of playmates. Should they escape those, then rickets stunted them or made them bow-legged, hence, 'He couldn't stop a pig in an entry.' Scurvy was rampant, marring many a pretty face and usually shewing up around the mouth, giving the skin the appearance of having been sandpapered. The boy who was never seen without the bandage covering his nose, or what was left of it, held in place by loops around his ears (my mother, ever the authority, said it was lupus) always walked fast, head down as if wishing to avoid other boys and their curiosity about his gruesome affliction. Does anyone get gumboils these days? Bulbous growths on the gums, quite painless and usually disappearing in a day or two. They were quite common and were believed to be caused by eating too much bread.

A Bishop of Liverpool, asked to allow the use of a Parish room as a day school for the children of the district, had this to say: 'The children from the surrounding district would be poor and this would harm the room for its other uses. You cannot have a school full of poor children without a very large quantity of dirt to say nothing of other things which poor children bring with them.'

That was before my time, but not much, and may give some idea of what we so-called slum-dwellers had to contend with.

CHAPTER FOUR

Tuppence in the Balcony, Penny in the Pit

The Saturday afternoon visit to the pictures was our one and only treat, twopence in the Balcony, penny in the Pit. Balcony patrons, as befitted their status, queued under a covered walkway, the Pit rabble submitting themselves to the open air. Attired in an ankle-length coat adorned with brass epaulettes and a gold-braided cap held in place by his ears, Old Soupy-Eyes, armed with a long cane, stands at the top of the steps, guarding the entrance to the Pit, now and then administering a thwack to some youngster attempting to break ranks. Up and down the queue shuffles the Chewing Gum man, 'Ere y'ar now,' he intones, 'everybody's doing it, everybody's chewing it, Wrigley's spearmint, five sticks a penny,' his doleful litany drowned in a rousing cheer as the projectionist is seen climbing the iron ladder to his box. Sounds of doors opening reach the ears of the waiting mob. Soupy-Eyes braces himself for the rush but he is swept aside, overwhelmed.

I honestly believe that no generation ever enjoyed the pictures as much as we did. Wrapped in the warmth of hundreds of young bodies, the tang of peeling oranges in our nostrils, we sat under the dust-laden beam of the projectionist's lamp in total darkness and in complete harmony with our idols on the screen. The airless cinema became a place of wonder: no sweet-wrappers rustled, no ice-cream sellers broke the spell; howls of derision greeted the occasional breakdown and when at times the screen appeared to dissolve in flames we knew it was all part of the magic.

Art Accord, William S. Hart, Hoot Gibson, Tom Mix, Lou Tellegan, J. Farrell McDonald (trapped in the miner's shack at the head of the canyon and aware that the posse was getting closer: 'Where was Moses when the light went out?' he said, dropping his smouldering corncob into the barrel of dynamite). These were our heroes. Then there was Mary Miles Minter, Nazimova of whom we sang a rather rude song, Louise Fazenda, Polly Moran and once a glimpse of the Divine Sarah Bernhardt, her wooden leg tucked out of sight and the Queen of them all, Pearl White, who had a song written about her:

> My little pearl of the army
> Pearl of the picture screen
> You're the Queen of the picture screen
> And the pride of the whole world too
> When the band plays Yankee Doodle
> Rule Britannia too
> There's many a lad would die to be glad
> For a pearl of a girl like you.

Anyway, that's what it sounded like in 1917.

Fatty Arbuckle, Ben Turpin, Chester Conklin and Larry Semon (who carried his own rock to hide behind when the Indians chased him), Buster Keaton and Stan Laurel, long before he met his Ollie, Billie Ritchie and Tarzan (Joe Bonomo).

> Oh the sun shines bright on Billie Ritchie
> His belly's itchy
> For the want of whisky
> And his kahki trousers they want mending
> Before we send him
> To the Dardanelles.

Of course there was no one quite like Charlie. Some have tried to find a message in his films but we didn't have to: the tough guy on Easy Street had his counterpart in any of the back streets of Scotland Road, the shabbily-dressed men and women, the mean houses were all too familiar and if the Copper didn't meet our standards, the lamp post, the preacher and Easy Street was us.

The pattern never changed, the News, the Big picture, the Serial and always a comedy. Serials such as *Judex* and *Trailed By Three* went on for sixteen weeks and when the hero seated at the roll-top writing desk had his wrists clamped in a vice-like grip by two skeleton hands appearing from nowhere we had to wait until the following Saturday to learn of his fate, and next Saturday was light years away. When the operator made the horses go over fences backwards we howled our delight, and there was the oft-repeated one reeler shewing the elderly professor scampering about the woods with a butterfly net, vainly attempting to catch his prey. We were convulsed at the idiocy of it, unaware that few, if any of us, would ever enter the comfortable world of the mad hunter.

The chief claim to fame of Felix the Cat was that he kept on walking. The black and white cartoon never appeared on our own picture house, so we had to make a special journey to the Gaiety in Scotland Road which normally we avoided as it ranked high on the list of flea pits. On Saturday afternoon it was bedlam, hordes of yelling kids chasing each other, clambering over the seats, dropping from the balcony, looking for fights, the female attendants immersed in their gossip knowing that the first flickerings of the screen would bring order to the mob they were powerless to control. Amidst all the mayhem the little mothers shepherded their baby sisters and brothers to the lav. Naturally, Felix had his own song. There were dozens of them, this is one:

> There's a funny little cat with a tummy nice and fat
> Felix is his name, he's won picture fame
> Got a funny little walk, whiskers on his chin
> And no matter where he goes or what occurs to him,
>
> (Chorus) Felix keeps on walking keeps on walking still.
>
> Cannibals then caught him, tasty bit they thought him
> Skinned him like a rabbit, he was so cut up until
> A nigger's scalp he noticed there
> stuck it on where he felt bare
> wagged his nothing in the air
> and he kept on walking still.

The reference to 'niggers' bothered us not a jot. Those were the attitudes of the times. Were we not members of an Empire covering half the world (or was it three quarters)?

To be taken to an evening performance, especially at the Second

House, was something to boast about. The better-off paid sixpence in the Balcony and wore hats and bowlers. Fourpence got you a seat in the Pit where shawls and flat caps were the vogue. During one manager's reign he would explain the Big picture at great length to the audience before it was screened, leaving out the denouement – all accepted without a murmur according to my mother. The patrons became utterly absorbed in a film and during a particularly heavy scene between villain and heroine the cinema became filled with loud exclamations of 'Yer bloody swine', 'God's curse on yer', 'Take no notice of him gerl', and similar heart-felt warnings. Sex was never anything more exciting than Nazimova or Theda Bara fluttering mascara-laden eyelashes whilst reclining half-dressed on a white bear-skin rug. Every film was a satisfying mixture of action, villainy, retribution and love. A happy ending was obligatory and men and women were never ashamed to weep.

I recall seeing a film at our local picture house based on the sinking of the Titanic. The First Class passengers are in full evening dress assemble, on the deck of the sinking liner, waiting to take their rightful places in such lifeboats as are available when suddenly the Black Gang, aware that they are in imminent danger of being scalded to death, suffocated or simply drowned, spew on to the deck to the consternation of the waiting passengers who are obviously mystified as to the identity of these apparitions, appalled and wondering where on earth they'd come from. At this point the young officer with the Jack Holt profile points his revolver at the rabble and utters the fateful words, 'Back, you scum!' at which the scum, realising they had made a faux pas, retreat to die a variety of unpleasant deaths, although not before one of them makes a cowardly dash for the lifeboats, leaving Jack Holt no choice but to shoot him neatly in the back.

The audience shewed their appreciation by breaking into wild applause, seemingly unaware that the scum thus portrayed were their husbands, sons, brothers, sweethearts. Being young and not wishing to be left out, I joined in the applause. I've no excuse except that Jack Holt was one of my film heroes.

After years of watching films I think that for sheer terror-filled emotion, the sight of the Four Horsemen of the Apocalypse, War, Famine, Pestilence and Death, skeleton riders surging off the screen into the blackness of the cinema and starring Rudolph Valentino has never been equalled. Wonderful, wonderful and all for a penny.

'Violin, Pianoforte and Theory', announced the brass plate outside the music teacher's house. Sallying forth to visit his pupils, umbrella tightly rolled, with his swaying, dignified walk and highly polished button-up boots (a proper little diddy man, my mother said) he looked what he was: a real gentleman and we gave him respect. The family must have been comfortably off because their son had everything, clasp knife, bicycle, well-off clothes, a boy scout uniform and boots with rubber heels.

Music lessons being low down on our parents' priority list it was not surprising that the street provided only one pupil, and that a reluctant one. We watched in secret glee as the budding violinist hid in the doorway of his house, hoping we hadn't seen him, then, thinking the coast was clear, dashing to the music teacher's a mere four doors away, followed by a rousing cheer from his tormentors emerging from the back entry. We were invited, one by one, into the music teacher's spotless parlour to put on headphones and hear for the first time the magic of wireless. It was 1922 I think, the station ZLO, and I am afraid we weren't very impressed: it seemed to be all violins, our preference being for the mouth-organ or the squeeze box (piano accordion). Later came the craze to build your own wireless set, the components being a six-inch square Bakelite board, a fragment of cobalt, a cat's whisker, a cotton-reel and a length of copper wire. This cost seven and sixpence, more than a day's wages for many, whilst headphones (Brandes) were twenty five shillings a pair, so having built your set you had to wait to borrow the only pair in the street. It was believed that putting them in the coal bucket amplified the sound.

The music teacher and his wife were warm-hearted people, often taking one of the street children to their holiday home, a wooden bungalow in Moreton-on-Wirral. A holiday was something new to me and when I was invited even the shock of the dry lavatory couldn't take away the fascination of the Cheshire countryside, the hedges, the grass, the birds, the cows and the sound of church bells drifting across the fields on the Sunday evening from the wonderfully named Saughall Massie. Pure Rupert Brooke.

At breakfast, the mother gently reproved me for cutting the top of my egg (you were supposed to crack it with a spoon you see) and I suppose I was given other lessons in deportment, but they were anything but snobs and I needed to learn. Although they were strict Church of England they arranged for the son to conduct me to the local Catholic church, but of that all I remember was its corrugated iron roof. With parents like that you would have expected the son to become a brain surgeon or something of the sort, but, boarding a bus some thirty years later, there he was, a cheerful it rather cynical bus conductor.

CHAPTER FIVE

Grandad, the Moneylender
& the Big House

The man standing on the corner of our street wasn't very impressed with his surroundings, debating in his mind whether the inhabitants were worthy of inclusion in the census and finally deciding to register the business people only, which is why, when Gores Directory appeared, a publication covering the whole of our great city, most of Scotland Road dwellers were left out. Perhaps he was tipped off by his superiors not to be too fussy: after all, the district was a rather dubious one.

Had Mary Ann McGuiness known that she was to be officially recognised as a business woman, she would have exposed her single tooth in a witch-like cackle echoed by howls of laughter from the resident cronies in the tiny shop where she sold fruit and vegetables rejected as unsaleable by the market men. Mary Ann had a double qualification, as she was the owner of the coal yard next door where for fourpence the local women could buy a quantity of slack shovelled, weighed and poured into their aprons by the proprietress herself.

Also in the census were the pawnbroker, the second-hand clothes dealer and the publican. My father, a coal hawker, wasn't entered but was unlikely to lose sleep over it. The householders went unrecognised, which was a pity for, with a few exceptions, they were a hard-working, compassionate and deeply religious people and you will not see their like again.

Such a one was Mick, a huge man and a dead ringer for Mack Sennet, setting out every morning carrying a massive shovel on his shoulder to join his fellow coal heavers on the Dock Road where, like obedient children, they formed a circle in the roadway to await the arrival of the Bowler-hatted Boss (The Blocker Man) stalking the circle to tap certain men on the shoulder indicating that they were 'on,' that is to say, taken on for work. At one o'clock they were discharged and were then required to form another circle with the rejects of the morning when the ritual was repeated. They did this every day.

We kids liked the coal heaver: he always gave us a cheerful smile, enhanced by the mask of coal dust. With six children, himself and his wife and only a single tap in the house it was remarkable how the family kept clean, but they did.

The woman who lay under the window, waving a feeble hand to us as we played in the street, had dropsy, according to my mother, a mine of information on death and diseases, ever ready to describe their effects in chilling detail. When the woman died, as we were confident she would, we lined up to see her in her coffin, a traditional practice and a mark of respect.

The coach-builder was a God-fearing man, his permanently pious expression indicating the calm confidence of a Christian with four aces. He served as an altar boy (altar man?) and occasionally as a runner for the priest on Sundays when collecting money from the faithful. His wife was a plump, gentle soul, living only for family and her spotless home. The youngest daughter, timid and doll-like would whisper her strange stories to me as we stood at her doorstep on a dark winter's evening, and though it was gratifying to be confided in I could never see her other than an innocent twelve-year-old as I was.

Winter's nights meant the coggy watchman with his coke-fed fire and his hut shaped like a coffin on end, guarding a hole in the ground. It drew us like a magnet and whilst revelling in the heat from the glowing brazier, we listened respectfully to the words of wisdom, which no coggie worth his salt ever failed to pass on to his audience. One, aware perhaps that he was in enemy territory, solemnly informed us that every night before going to bed he and his wife stood to attention and sang 'God Save the King', which impressed us greatly although we couldn't see such a commendable practice finding favour in Scotland Road.

***

Towards six o'clock each night Old Grandad the labourer came home pushing his handcart laden with second-hand bricks, shovels and assorted tools of the building trade, his dungaree trousers stiff with accumulations of brick-dust plaster and cement. A lifetime of slogging hard work had given him a permanent stoop and distorted his hands into twin clusters of fingers, thumbs and knuckles. We helped him heave his handcart over the pavement and into the lock-up and the gentle old man smiled his thanks.

We were very fond of Grandad and on the summer evening when they came to collect him we left our games and laughed delightedly when he announced from the steps of the fever van that he was going on his holidays. But Old Grandad never came back from his holidays and one more insignificant human departed the scene and left us to our games.

It too was on a summer evening that the landau and its tired-looking nag parked at the corner of our street attracted the attention of a small crowd conspicuous by the poverty of their appearance. The two occupants, red-faced, corpulent and jolly-looking, gazed out at the gawping citizens with mild amusement. The one with the frock coat and the snuff scattered down the front of his vest was T. P. O'Connor, Tay Pay, as he was affectionately called and our local M.P. to boot, his companion none other than our own dear Canon. The tiny crowd gazed back in admiration, nay, adoration, thrilled to be so close to such popular figures, waiting for one of them to say something, hopefully something humorous which they could relay back to their families or workmates but sadly nothing came. Eventually our Canon heaved himself up and gave the assembled throng his blessing, causing some confusion as the blessed scrambled for the available kneeling space on the pavement.

Memory of that scene came when I was much older and with it the realisation that both men were drunk. To have harboured such thoughts then would have risked losing my immortal soul but being older, I was able to withstand the shock.

John the Cowkeeper was a Yorkshire man, a 'yowk', my father called him, by which I suppose he meant a yokel, living alone in a house empty of family, pictures, floor covering or comforts of any kind. The shippen which housed his six cows was directly under our back bedroom and looking down on them through a knothole in the floorboards we could feel the heat rising from their bodies.

As a child I would toddle round to John's dairy to get a warm drink straight from the cow and to watch him cooling the milk which he poured through a funnel into a steel ventilator, from which it emerged through the vanes directly into the churns. This operation required a bucket of hot water into which I promptly sat only to he rushed off to my mother bawling my head off. When I became older I sometimes helped on his rounds. That was when housewives bought milk straight from the churn and a valued possession was a white quart jug. One time he had a real high-stepper of a pony which would stand in the street harnessed and docile as a lamb until it heard the key turn in the padlock, at which point it would tear off like something possessed, with old John hurling himself into the float and grabbing the reins just in time.

There was a morning when, standing in the float with ten-gallon churn of milk, the sound of the padlock hit the mad moke's ears and off it shot. Grabbing the reins instinctively, I tugged on the wrong one and there we were, careering along the pavement, one wheel on, one wheel off. Fortunately the Cowkeeper, with an extra spurt and his usual acrobatics, brought the pony under control at the same time giving me a stinging crack on the head and a warning not to do that again. We were lucky – the main road was only yards away.

On another day John and I, armed with long canes, drove three of his poor dried-up cows through the streets onto the luggage boat and into the Lairage at Birkenhead. The pride I felt in this exercise excluded any pity for the animals but it's as well I didn't witness their ignoble end, as according to John they were stunned with a sledgehammer and then cut up.

The Boy Scouts marched through our street every other Sunday coming from the Black Church, the St Martins-in-the-Fields burial ground for victims of a cholera epidemic of the previous century. Carried away by the sound of the band playing 'Off to the Russian War, Boys', and by the uniform, I persuaded the son to introduce me to his Scoutmaster as a potential recruit but, on learning I was a Catholic, the kindly man regretted that be could not accept me. My first lesson in religious discrimination.

The Moneylender, alas I knew her well, may she rest in peace. Grim-faced, unrelenting and contemptuous of her clients, able to transport us to the heights of delight or oblige us to swallow the bitter pill of refusal. I suppose my father must have given my mother some sort of subsistence from his coal round, nevertheless she was forever short of money. 'I just can't make 'ens meat,' she said, a statement which puzzled me for a while until the penny dropped. As a result, part of my childhood was spent making trips every Saturday to the moneylender to beg for a loan of five shillings or ten or an extension of the current loan. If conditions were favourable I was to ask for a pound, but this wasn't very often. What with the interest, half a crown in the pound, the period of the loan, the state of the existing loan and other factors it could become so convoluted that I often returned home in tears to have it explained again and my mother had an extremely short temper.

How I hated it, darting up the back entry to escape the knowing stares of the neighbours before confronting the Gorgon in the gloomy kitchen where she conducted her business. The success of the operation meant that I got a penny for the pictures which began at three o'clock, so it was a situation fraught with anxiety, particularly if the negotiations became protracted. Sometimes I made it just as old Soupy-Eyes was about to slam the doors, other times the show went on without me.

Towering over the little houses was a blackened hulk of a building, the Big House we called it, harbouring Mary-Ann's coalyard and green-grocery store, four families so wretched in their poverty that the rest of the street found it hard to acknowledge their existence, plus assorted vermin. Therein lived Paddy the coin tosser, forerunner of George Raft, his father, like Paddy, stunted and nondescript. And then there were the Tudors, holders of a right royal name, the head of the house accepting without question his soldier's reward of a verminous hovel, a quarter-share in a lavatory which often overflowed generously into the street and the burden of a hunch-back son for whom there was never any hope, medical or otherwise.

The Big House also gave shelter to Big Annie, tall and muscular, her graying hair stretched into a tight bun, one eye covered in a white film, adding to an already fearsome appearance. Attired in shawl, blouse, Lindsay petticoats and men's boots she sat at the entrance to her 'home' muttering curses to herself and passers-by alike. She had been known to tear off her blouse and fight like a man and when the police took her in (though not without a struggle) the accommodation they provided must surely have seemed superior to her own. We never knew her real name. She was Big Annie to us, a touchy character and one to steer clear of. Her generation had tales to tell of the famine in Ireland, of epidemics, bitter strikes, the great days of sailing ships and the days, few in number perhaps, when she was young and happy. If only we could have approached them and heard their stories. I like to think that this outrageous lady was once a pretty girl, loved and desired by a handsome lad, a sailor perhaps, wanting to marry her. Poor Annie, the lowest of the lowest of the low, just one of the many women referred to contemptuously as handcart women, or Mary-Ellens, scraping a living from the sale of fruit and vegetables from a handcart which they trundled out to the suburbs, their only protection against the weather being a heavy paisley shawl. None ever wore a hat and their crowning glory was an abundance of waist-length jet-black hair, like that possessed by the woman who parked her handcart in our yard. Somewhere in the depths of the Big House lived another family of which I have no recollection and to them l offer my apologies.

The Da was gaunt, lanky, sandy-moustached and solemn. His lanyard, bell bottoms and sailor's hat might have suggested that he was a sailor, except that he worked on the liners and to be a real sailor, in my opinion, you had to be on a battleship, a cause of much dispute between me and members of his family. Their house was a two-storied structure and from the garret to the slime-covered cellar where Auntie Annie operated a laundry it was squalid. Playing in the garret, our other companions were fleas, gray repulsive things roughly about the size of ladybirds and too big to be despatched in the customary manner between one's thumb nails. Whether they came from Da's bunk in the bowels of his White Star liner or from Auntie's laundry they had found a comfortable home.

Da's family worshipped him and when the sailor was home from the sea it was fascinating watching the old salt picking pieces from a cooked pig's head, his drooping moustache festooned with strands of succulent pork whilst around him his adoring offspring waited patiently for titbits. Fortunately for me it was strictly a family orgy and I was never offered any. The eldest of his brood of nine had 'ideas.' 'I was walking to my seat in the Empire,' she was reported as saying, 'when my suspender broke. l was terribly embarrassed.' Hearing this we howled, not at the catastrophe but the word embarrassed: it was posh and a stranger to our vocabulary. She was bent on becoming a lady, bless her, and I hope she succeeded.

I had occasion to belt one of the clan silly on learning he had hit my young sister, chasing him through back streets and back entries before catching him. When l returned to the street l was met by Auntie Annie, her goitrous eyes bulging more fiercely than ever as she handed her snivelling nephew a stick, then stood over him whilst he beat me unmercifully. l refused to cry even when a neighbour came to my rescue. l did that later in the bare back bedroom with only the picture of Michael Collins to see me and the cows below to hear me.

Alongside their house was a passage and at the end, its door hanging on one hinge, was the lavatory. Through the keyhole at the other end we were often entertained when one of the girls occupied the throne and a capacious affair it was, for whilst her face was lost behind her knees her rear was submerged to her neck and there she sat, crooning to herself, long enough for us to get bored and seek mischief elsewhere.

Amongst the residents were a baker, a coal heaver, a sailor, a music teacher, a navvy, a coach builder, a cooper, a milkman, a publican, a greengrocer, two dockers, a market porter, a purser (very elegant) a carter and a clerk. We also had our full quota of war widows thanks to Sir Douglas Haigh and his pals of the Vitai Lampada generation. The men were stern, unbending characters, seldom acknowledging us as we played in the street. Machismo there was in full, dignity was everything: to ignore it was to invite trouble.

l wish you could have seen the sisters Lizzie and Cissie, sixty or more years old, dressed in black bombazine, spotless white aprons, lace collars adorned with a cameo brooch and beautifully polished button-up boots. They stood at the door of their neat little house laughing with delight at our antics at play, two delightful old ladies perhaps from some remote Welsh hamlet. Kilvert would have recognised them immediately. Straight out of the nineteenth century they were, and how they ever came to live in Scotland Road was a mystery.

There were a number of widows in the street, the result of the recent carnage, of accidents, or disease, anthrax being by no means uncommon, caused by handling raw hides at the docks or the tanyards. Chest infections were the lot of cotton porters and the sugar refineries had their own brand of horrors, such as multiple boils and horrific skin diseases.

Georgina (we were supposed to be sweethearts) was the youngest of three daughters of a war widow. Her sisters worked in a bag warehouse converted from a mill (ancient and dignified, it was demolished at the first opportunity by idiot planners) and how clean and neat they looked as they hurried to and from their work, never stopping to speak to anyone. l stood with Georgina one evening as she complained in a petulant voice at the way they were, 'Going on in there', nodding her pretty head towards the house where one of her sisters lay dead of consumption with the mother being comforted by the neighbours. In a few short weeks my poor Georgina was herself a victim. Her face, her deep-set eyes and dark ringlets are as clear to me as it it were yesterday. Thirteen was too young to die.

A couple of women lived 'over the brush.' Nellie seemed happy with her fancy-man although my mother said he was sly and not to be trusted; a sleveen she called him. Her son Tommy, nicknamed Hearty (we never asked why), was a sad figure with a wheezy chest enduring a dog's life from his mother and her man. He wasn't very bright at school and couldn't fight to save his life. Instead he would try to bluster his way out of trouble, which only made us laugh. After school and at weekends he sold newspapers and like all newspaper lads he was always in a mad rush so if you hadn't got your penny ready he would tear off, shouting, 'On the double tomorrow!' Our two evening papers were the *Echo* and the *Express*, the latter always referred to as 'the Exy', and Exy Cosher was our affectionate name for all paper lads. Bigger and heavier than today's papers, they cost ninepence a dozen, thirteen to the dozen, so to make a shilling it meant selling three dozen. For the stunted, underfed lads carrying two dozen or more on a wet winter's evening, knowing they couldn't go home until the last one was sold, life was indeed grim.

On an evening when my mother took the paper from Tommy she remarked that he looked ill. 'He said his chest was paining,' she said. Within a week he was dead. He was fourteen. How Tommy enjoyed telling us about the delicious conny-onny butties he would sneak: a piece of bread smeared with condensed milk, the highlight of his day.

* * *

Scotland Road, 1908

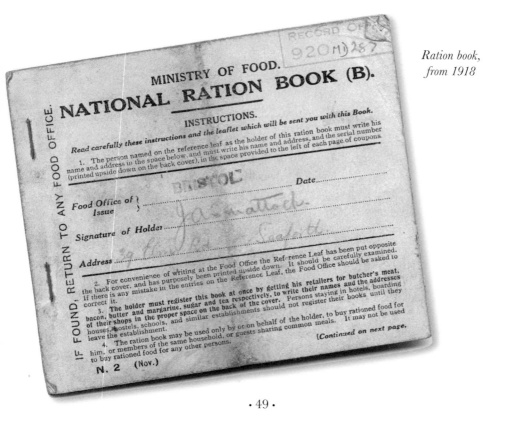

Ration book, from 1918

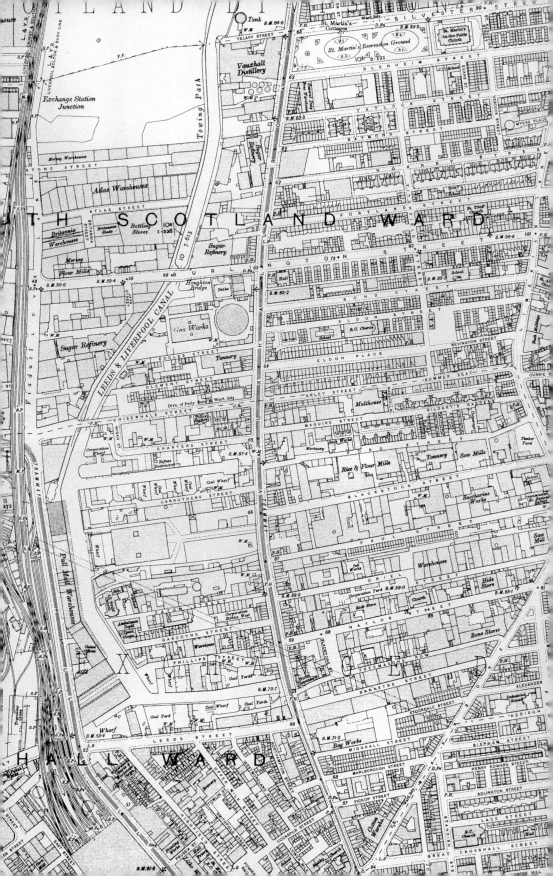

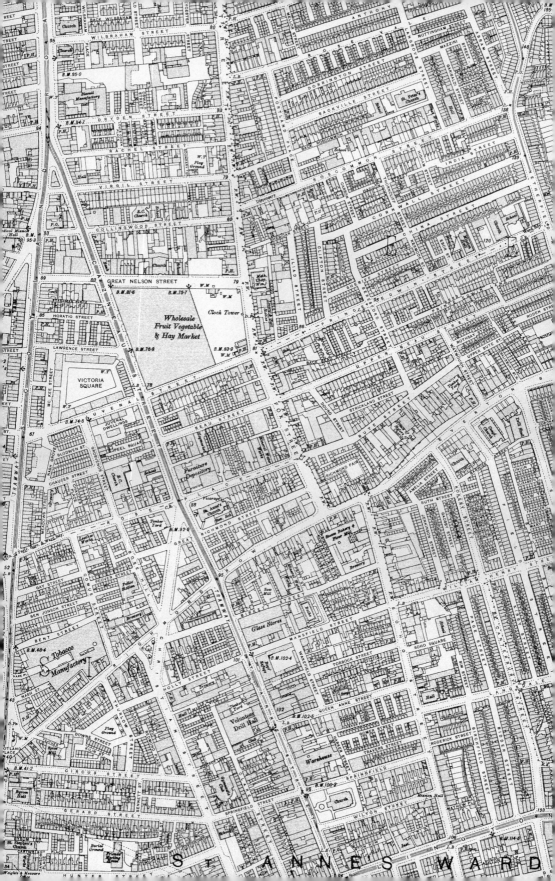

Carter, with horse and wagon

Previous page: map of Scotland Road and surrounding areas, c. 1906.
Reproduced courtesy of Alan Godfrey Maps

A motor-run tram, 1915

An electric tram, 1905

Co-operative store on Cowley Road

Police strike, 1919

The site of the Adelphi Hotel, 1912

Evidence of looting after the police strike

*Small boy carrying
jugs of beer*

Newspaper boys

Lime Street Station, 1890

Kiosk under the railway arches, selling Fry's Chocolate

Langdale Street pub

Corner shop on Dickson Street

A group of slum children, 1920

The slum of Boundary Terrace

Corner of Eldon Street and Vauxhall Road, 1905

Ben Johnson Street

Pub on Limekiln Lane

Market in Liverpool

Arches at George's Dock site

George's Docks, 1901

The front of court-houses in Lace Street

Below: residents of Clayton Street

The foregoing catalogue of occupations does not include that of my father, a coal hawker. The sign on his cart which also adorned the yard gates said, 'Coal Merchant,' rather optimistically I thought. When he disappeared, leaving a mound of debts, I as a young man found myself urging a weary, reluctant nag through the dismal streets, shouting in an uncertain voice, 'One and Nine Coal,' aware that a rival behind me was doing the same except that his coal was One and Seven (a cwt).

> Over here in England I'm helpin' wid the hay,
> And I wisht I was in Ireland The live long day;
> Weary on the English Hay and Sorra take the wheat
> Och! Corrymeela an' the blue sky over it.

The upholsterer was an exiled Irishman, passionate in argument, tenaciously Catholic and homesick for the sights and sounds of his Kathleen Ni Houlihan. Unable to find regular work he drank heavily and was violent to his family, so that life in that two-up, two-down must have been hellish. One son stammered so badly that in his agonised attempts to form words he would quite literally push you off the pavement. The eldest son bore the brunt of his father's frustrations, his face taut with anger as he spoke of his hatred for him. He was determined to get away, keeping us informed of how much he had saved in order to emigrate. I waved him goodbye as he sailed away on the S.S. *Baltic* for the States. It was 1928. We wrote to each other for a while. Once he sent me a copy of the *New York Daily News*, which had on its front page a photo of Ruth Snyder smiling through the bars of her prison cell, from which she was later escorted to the electric chair. It was 1948 before I saw him again. Still drawn and grey-faced, he had never taken to New York. 'If you collapse in the street they walk over you,' he said. By then his father was dead but the hatred lingered.

Mr Eden was a carter; he and his wife were my favourite people, their up-country accents shewing they came from somewhere the other side of Aintree, a good five miles away. They were childless and I would sit on their doorstep trying to attract sympathy by looking forlorn, much to the amusement of Mrs Eden, whose merry laugh and offer of a jam butty were enough to wipe the woebegone expression from my face.

Seated on a pile of provender sacks on Mr Eden's wagon I watched his strong hands steering the great Shire horse through streets where metal plates fixed to the wall shewed the way to docks with names like Collingwood, Canada, Wellington, Clarence and Bramley-Moore. Lads ran alongside pleading for a ride and when we took our place in the long line of wagons waiting to enter the docks and Mr Eden gave me a drink of tea from the lid of his blue enamel tea-can, I felt a real grown-up.

Carters were a race apart, employed by team owners such as George Davies, whose stables housed scores of magnificent horses. The docks were the fulcrum of their lives. They were the only people my father seemed to know, their talk being of swollen fetlocks and greasy heels and things like the Staggers and the Strangles. Hours spent with curry comb and dandy brush shewed in the gleaming coats of their horses, harness brasses polished and shining, all combined to create a good turnout.

On Sunday mornings, sporting their best scarves, they made their way to the stables to feed and water their charges and on Bank Holidays they would exercise them in the surrounding streets, giving the children an opportunity to ride on the massive beasts, their delight tempered by nervous glances at the cobble stones far below.

CHAPTER SIX

Ma, Da &
the Black Gang

'My mother always seemed a fairy princess
a dark lithe figure, appearing of another
texture, radiant, translucent, intense, a
diamond star in her hair its lustre dimmed
by the flashing glory of her eyes.'

Winston Churchill

I never knew my mother, Mary, not to have a job of some sort, always
a menial one, in cafés, hotels or the harsh discipline of a workhouse
laundry where she started working at 7 am and where conversation
was forbidden until her quota of linen was ironed and inspected, which
could take most of the day. There she was, an expert laundress, married
to a man who after his wedding day never wore a collar again in his life.
She worked in one hotel notable for its high jinks on Grand National
night, smuggling out sweet wafer biscuits and part-eaten carcasses of
chickens. When these occupations weren't available she scrubbed floors.

She was twelve when her mother died, leaving seven young children
and, following the practice of those days, they were separated, never to
meet as a family again. Dr Barnardo's despatched two of the boys to
Canada, no doubt to suffer the horrors which many of those children
experienced at the hands of rapacious farmers. Later on, with an older
sister, she joined the Order of the Little Sisters of the Poor and was sent
to Paris, where 'We got up at five o'clock, attended Mass and after a
bowl of gruel walked the streets begging for alms. If we were late getting

back we had to kneel on the stone floor until given permission to rise.' Her sense of humour never deserted her. 'Allez a la cuisine and shushey le dooley,' she recalled being told, her version of, 'Go to the kitchen and find some milk.'

Still a novice, she arrived back in England with a party of nuns to open a branch on the outskirts of Liverpool where, deciding convent life was not for her, she retired. After that it was domestic service in the houses of sea captains in the south end of the city and in doctors' houses in Rodney street, 2/6d a week all found. Where and how she met my father l don't know, nor did she ever speak of it.

There are some who speak with pride of having been brought up in a two-up two-down dwelling: ours was a one-down two-up with a yard and stable attached, having accommodation for four horses. We never had more than one.

We grew up with lamps and candles. Every night my mother cleaned the smoke-blackened funnel of the lamp with newspaper before breathing on it and giving it a final polish. She then trimmed the lamp wick of its crust of carbon, finally topping up with paraffin oil. Water had to be carried from a tap fixed to the wall of the midden and if the horse got there first you had to wait until it withdrew its mouth from the tap. It froze every winter and you can imagine (or perhaps not) what it was like getting ready for school whilst waiting for the tap to be unfrozen. Once a year the midden was sprayed a brilliant white by a happy-go-lucky pair from the Health Department, operating a Heath Robinson contraption, one turning an enormous wheel with his mate spraying the limewash. Despite these precautions, when the weather got really hot and tar bubbled in the streets, the midden spawned thousands of white maggots and it was a heart-stopping experience coming through the wicket gate to be confronted by a seething mass of the loathsome creatures extending right across the yard. Luckily they never made for the house.

Sitting on the lavatory could be interesting too when a rat, emerging from a hole by the door, would change its mind when it spotted you. They usually kept to the stable but sometimes one would gnaw its way via the skirting board into the living room to be met by our ferocious tomcat, grisly encounters witnessed by my mother and described fully the next day.

This was the house my mother struggled with for so many years:

of her eleven children, seven failed to survive babyhood and to come downstairs in the morning and see a tiny coffin on trestles was part of our childhood. At twelve o'clock when we came from school, the coffin and its tiny occupant would be gone. As an infant I contracted pneumonia three times, as well as the Spanish flu (me, Lillian Gish and half of Europe). On the last occasion, when the doctor decided I was 'a goner,' she wrapped me in all the clothes she could find, put on her shawl and walked to the Pier Head where she plodded up and down the Landing Stage for hours praying incessantly before returning home where I then ate like a horse. She gave all the credit to God and the sea air.

She was a fervent Socialist, hating the inequalities of the times and, despite her very English name of Watts, was well versed in Irish politics, holding forth on the rebellions, Wolfe Tone, Robert Emmett ('Faithful companion, he died with a smile,' she sang), De Valera and Michael Collins. She canvassed for the Labour party in a district reeking with hatred of anything Catholic, the inhabitants believing that the Labour party harboured too many of that creed. Knowing its badly-lit streets and its reputation, it must have required great courage to do what she did.

As she was invariably at work, my two sisters and myself had to fend for ourselves. Any food was locked away and money was left (3½d) for four cakes to be bought at Mrs Woods' corner shop, where sage, mint, parsley and dried bloaters hanging from the ceiling shared the fumes from the paraffin oil tank in the corner. This was our dinner, mine being the lemon cheese, with the fourth divided as fairly as possible. With no fire in the grate there was no way of making tea so we drank water or nothing. There were jobs to do, setting the fire, washing the floor, making the beds and cleaning the fire irons with emery paper, the sharp edges of the fender catching between my thumb and forefinger: very painful. If there was a baby in the house, and there usually was (in the care of a completely dotty relative with a vile temper and an appalling squint) then milk had to be brought from a depot in Holly street, run for the benefit of poor families. On the way l managed a quick peep at the Police Gazette in a newsagents window, shewing horrendous drawings of wardens, execution sheds and gallows.

At one time, the family fortunes had sunk so low that we were reduced to applying for food coupons from the Parish, a move widely regarded as the last stop before the workhouse. Twice a week in the dinner hour I collected the handouts at a mission hall. Came the day when the queue of mendicants was longer than usual and, weighed down with a yard-long loaf and other comestibles intended to sustain us for a few days, I realised I was late for school. The headmaster, meeting me on the stairs, listened patiently to the tearful incoherences of a blubbering lad and arranged for me to escape punishment. And from the bottom of my heart my belated thanks to the woman who shewed such Christian sympathy on the day when, coming from the mission, I experienced an overwhelming urge 'to go', brought on by the frantic pace of dinner time and she allowed me to use her lavatory, outside of course. Of such incidents are memories made. The Mission is still there, like the river, silent and abandoned.

***

Bear with me whilst l tell the following tale. In the days before chem-ical fertilisers, horse manure was a valuable commodity, with farmers paying up to sixteen shillings a load, collected. It came about that our midden, packed with organic goodies, became the target of a local wide boy aware of its value and aware that my father would be absent for seven days. Late one evening my mother surprised the villain skulking around the midden and promptly rushed him off the premises, at which point he began to threaten her. The main road was only a few yards away, and approaching a policeman she asked for assistance. He cut short her explanation saying, 'Get off home you f— cow!' Now believe it or not, we weren't used to that sort of language: good old fashioned swearing yes, but not obscenity. it was regarded as a sin and rarely heard except perhaps during a drunken row. It was plain that this bobby firmly believed that the locals were an ignorant rabble. My mother decided he should learn otherwise.

The following day, wearing her best hat and shawl, she made her stand at Rose Hill Police Station, requesting to see the top man. The desk tried to persuade her to go away and given the merest excuse they would have put her inside, but she kept her cool and eventually was allowed to see the man in charge, who agreed to make inquiries.

Thus, one fine Sunday morning, I stared wide-eyed as a very large police inspector accompanied by an equally large sergeant came to our door and proceeded to gravely apologise for the conduct of the young policeman. 'He's young,' the Inspector said, the sergeant nodding in agreement, 'and he hasn't been in the Force very long.' However, he was prepared to take it further if she insisted. They appeared relieved when she agreed to drop the matter, not without declaring, as she often did, that the people of Scotland Road were decent human beings and entitled to respect.

They thanked her for being so understanding and left. It had been a brave thing to do and I suppose they were impressed. Policing methods in Scotland Road were rarely questioned. I remember seeing a policeman subdue a man by banging his head repeatedly on a water grid, and my mother was aware that she could become a marked woman. I wonder, did they put a special guard on the manure by way of compensation?

Well into her eighties she was still working, travelling daily to the suburbs where she 'did' for a family, as well as taking care of the old lady of the house, years younger than herself. I called at this house one day to take her home and she was called from the kitchen, where she was dealing with the debris of a Christmas dinner (for such was the day), using her Christian name in true servant fashion. Remembering her bright enquiring mind, her love of discussion and her courage I felt anger that she should be treated in such a fashion though I don't think it bothered her much: she had her independence – more important to her than anything else. She asked for nothing from anyone and any regrets she may have had for ambitions unfulfilled had long since faded.

She was ninety-four when she died, peacefully, in her own little home with my brother holding her hand. I refused to see her dead, preferring to remember her as she used to be, laughing, arguing, irreverent, holding her glass of Guinness (a life-long favourite), dismissing some pompous political figure with a tut of contempt, the same contempt she expressed for people who never attempted to improve themselves intellectually. 'Mix with people who can teach you something,' was her constant exhortation, and how pleased she was when I visited her with someone who measured up to her standards.

The relatives were annoyed when I admitted that I hadn't called the priest to give her the last rites but I didn't want her to see, in her last moments, a black-garbed figure muttering some mumbo-jumbo whose only effect would be to make her aware that she was dying. I'm glad I didn't. I like to believe that her final dreams were of days bathed in sunshine when she was young and innocent beyond the imaginings of today's young people. Anyway, how absurd to suggest that she, for whom almost every day of her life had meant struggle and hardship, should need some prayer-ridden formula to allow her to enter the Heaven in which she so fervently believed.

* * *

Although he had a reputation as a hard man my father, James Joseph Callaghan, never beat us. A sudden movement towards the brass-buckled belt holding up his corduroys was enough to bring us into line; my mother, though, would beat the daylights out of us even into our teens.

As a young man employed as a farrier he must have shod hundreds of carthorses, donkeys and ungovernable mules. The car and the lorry had yet to appear and these beasts of burden were the only means of transport by road. It was hot, sweaty work, not without danger, as he discovered when a donkey kicked his eye out. 'I felt it running down my cheek,' he said. 'But a donkey,' I thought, 'the indignity of it. Why couldn't it have been a carthorse?' Sitting opposite him at the table, watching the muscles of his face twitching as he munched his food, I wondered what lay behind the pink eye-shade. On the one occasion when I did catch a glimpse, there wasn't the hole through which could be seen the inside of his head, as I expected, but just a dark gray mass as if the socket had been filled with discarded chewing gum.

At twenty years of age, when for a short period I was obliged to work for him on his coal round (unpaid), our conversation never exceeded more than a dozen words, which may explain why even at that age I had never answered him back.

Some thirty years before he was born, Liverpool had become the unwilling host to those starving peasants fleeing the famine in Ireland, his father amongst them. They settled in a district already described as narrow, verminous, filthy and beset by vice. Thus was born Scotland Road. In this place my father grew up. From scraps of information he let fall I learnt that his father came from Shercock in County Cavan, his mother – her name was Strachan – from Scotland. Mothers died young those days but my grandfathers were still alive when we were children, although we never met them. One was in Kirkdale Homes, which sounded a cosy sort of place but was in fact a workhouse.

After the War, having lost his coal round, he was out of work for a long time until he got himself signed on the S.S. *Baltic* (the Hell Ship) as a trimmer, joining the Black Gang – the stokers, firemen, trimmers and greasers recruited from the Scotland Road area, recognised by the black shiny cap and scarf they wore and the kit bag of the same material containing their requirements for the trip.

As a trimmer, my father would be regarded at sea and at shore as the lowest form of life, but in 1920 work was hard to find. The munitions factories had disgorged thousands of redundant workers onto the streets; newspapers reported ex-officers standing in the gutters selling matches, laces, anything to survive. As an expert in the art of shovelling coal he probably thought he could handle it. It was an experience he was never to forget. Stripped to the waist, smothered in sweat and coal dust, arms racked by the loose steel deck plates, he pushed a heavy iron barrow laden with coal from the bunkers to the voracious furnaces, harassed and cursed at by bellowing, foul-mouthed stokers. The heat, the stink of oil, the clanging of the great steel doors closing on the furnaces all combined to make it the closest thing to Hell imaginable. It was brutal and degrading work; little wonder that when returning to their slum homes and the hovels of the courts they sought the garish lights and the sleazy comfort of the alehouses. A few days of drinking, fighting and carousing, then the sullen return to the backbreaking toil of the stoke-hold.

The extraordinary range of obscenities uttered by the Black Gang impressed my father but his indignation was reserved for the barber in New York who charged him a dollar (five shillings) for a haircut, fifteen times the price charged by Joe Grundy in Scotland Road. That first trip was his last and at five feet tall and one-eyed who could blame him.

In Scotland Road, where masculinity was all, my father took a quiet pride in his strength and it must have surprised the police sergeant, who had to use all his efforts to pin the little man, still fighting, against the midden wall before putting the handcuffs on him, the sequel to one of the many domestic crises we lived through and something I witnessed in tearful horror.

I never knew him to give us a birthday present, a Christmas gift or a word of advice or encouragement, which is why the memory of the ha'penny he gave on leaving for the War still remains. Apart from his pipe and the foul thick twist he smoked, his sole enjoyment was the weekly visit to the cinema. I'd watch him getting ready, wrapping his scarf around his neck and threading it through his braces before setting off. I followed, pleading to be taken with him. The cinema was just across the road and I would follow him right up to the pigeon hole and there, with a derisive grin, he'd put down his fourpence, say 'One,' and disappear into the blackness of the Pit.

Reflecting on those childhood days certain things become clear, such as the drudgery inflicted on my eldest sister, long domiciled in Australia and extremely happy I'm glad to say. She so often she was the butt of my mother's anger, with no way to appeal to an uncaring Father, her young life a perpetual grind of household chores and the care of younger children. God knows how she coped with school and cane-obsessed teachers.

She and I were sent out selling coal-bricks, nine inch squares of compressed coal dust and slack and filthy to handle. This was after school and because I insisted on pushing the handcart, my sister, twelve or thirteen at the time, had to do the donkey work, literally, between the shalls.

Some people tried to persuade us to leave the coal bricks, promising to pay later, others took pleasure in chasing us away. The bricks were three ha'pence each, or two for twopence ha'penny and we hatched a scheme whereby when two were sold separately for three ha'pence each: we said they were sold at two for twopence ha'penny. With the halfpenny we bought, and we never bought anything else, a bar of Fry's Creamy Chocolate, divided evenly and tasting heavenly despite its layer of coal dust. There was a price to pay for this behaviour of course, the guilty knowledge that we had broken at least two of the Ten Commandments: 'Thou shalt not steal' and 'Honour thy father and thy mother.' Her Benny had nothing on us.

The year was 1922 when we had the Prize Day, the first ever I believe, bringing a whiff of Greyfriars and The Firth Form at St Dominic's. The headmaster's table was piled high, the partitions drawn back to allow all of the Big Boys to witness the ceremony. Five times I went up for prizes, each time I chose a book and when I got home proud and happy my father uttered one word – 'Fluke.'

Writing this I feel sad, perhaps more than I did on that rather crushing day long ago. Did it bring home to him how much he lacked even the skimpy education I was getting? For him and his kind, schooling in the 1880s cost fivepence a week, a lot of money to find and no doubt the cause of much absenteeism.

When the little man died, having never kissed his children, used a telephone or ridden in a car, and having for most of his life gazed on to his little world out of one eye, away from his funeral hearse I sobbed bitterly, thinking on the past and his treatment of us. In spite of everything, we gave him respect. He was after all our father; it was his due. I did not feel any resentment towards him, even when told by my mother that he had left what money he possessed to the Church to have his name placed in the Book of Remembrance buried under the foundation stone of the new Catholic Cathedral.

CHAPTER SEVEN

Last Days at School

The time had come to leave Standard VI and the teacher who had given us a glimpse into the world of poetry and literature. I was sorry to leave. There was much to remember, such as the spontaneous cheer that went up when the Headmaster announced that in future we would visit the local swimming baths once a week, for free. We rarely missed the baths on Saturday morning: it cost a penny and included a towel and the chance to lie in the footbath, a receptacle about six feet square holding, if l remember, six boys head to tail wallowing in the luxury of warm water no more than a foot deep. I remember John Alden reading a passage from the New Testament, 'Made the Pharisee 'Fyst twast a week,' and neither threats nor coaxing could get him to say it otherwise. I remember the School Inspector asking me, amongst others, my ambition on leaving school and myself replying, 'The checker,' which was the nearest I could get to 'the Chancellor of the Exchequer.' And always I will remember the vacant place of the boy whose father had that morning met his fate at the nearby gaol at the official hour of eight o'clock, a half-crazed veteran of the trenches who, it was said, after a drinking bout, would squat behind a chair with a broom-handle, imitating the action of a machine gun. The victim was his wife, a simple handcart woman. Years later I passed their daughter in the street: I had known her quite well and would have liked to have spoken to her but the agony of her childhood experience shewed in her eyes and I walked on.

So to Standard VII, incorporating Ex-Seven, the fourteen year-olds due to leave school at the summer holidays, although the first Monday after leaving would find them at work and holidays merely a fond remembrance of school days.

With their education completed and anxious to embark on their careers, a wide variety of occupations was open to the boys from Ex-Seven: billiard marker; page boy; errand boy; hotter-upper in the shipyards; learner navvy in the Corporation; points lad (diverting the trams); Exy-cosher and, lowest of all occupations, can lad with the Army or the Navy – a last desperate resort.

Should your parents have the right sort of connections, Protestant or Catholic, you might become an apprentice fitter, joiner, cooper, wheelwright or, most glamorous of all, an office boy. Jobs for life in the Post Office, the trams or the railways could be had with a letter from the Holy Ghost, or so the locals claimed, otherwise easy jobs were reserved for sons and nephews.

Religion was an important factor when applying for work, some firms advertising that no Catholic need apply, as was the case with a well-known tobacco firm operating right in the middle of Scotland Road. One youth with an ambition to work at the Docks was tipped off that a certain Blocker Man was 'one of us', and to make the sign of the Cross when enquiring about a job, that on being told that no vacancies existed the Blocker Man emphasised the point by imitating the playing of a flute. Most unskilled jobs lasted until the boy reached sixteen, when his employer was obliged to pay insurance and unemployment stamps, resulting in the lad being dismissed without explanation. Nobody complained: it was all part of the system.

Charged with completing our education was a blue-chinned, tweedy dresser, very handy with the cane and an ego to withstand the blows from a jackhammer. Once, when I described a lion as sitting on its haunches, his lip curled like the brim on a bowler hat as he snarled, 'Lions don't sit like that!' at the same time failing to tell me that lions were found in the jungle. Personally, I don't think he knew.

Blue Chin made me a monitor, cleaning the blackboard, filling the inkwells (including those enlivened by a pinch of carbide, causing the ink to bubble and run all over the desk), going for new canes – the whippy ones so beloved of the teachers – and disposing of faded flowers, daffodils mostly, at the midden, which adjoined the lavatories and combined with the hideous doorless structures to produce the most appalling smells.

When the Headmaster commandeered me to write out dinner-tickets for the children whose parents were too poor to provide them with a dinner, I mentioned this system to my mother and, never one to miss an opportunity, she made me apply for this dubious privilege. Thus I became a dinner-hour kid. We had to walk more than a mile to a scowling industrial school where, after saying Grace, we were given a bowl of skilly, a bright yellow soup made of Indian corn with the consistency of wallpaper paste. I can't recall the taste but I know I ate the lot, after all I was only eleven with a perpetual hunger. You might think we were a bunch of merry schoolboys banging plates and joshing each other. You would be mistaken: we entered quietly, sat quietly, ate whatever was given to us and departed without a word. Being the objects of charity had that effect on us.

Why do I so clearly remember at that school seeing a boy down a gloomy corridor, stretching his hand out to be caned, just the two of them, the teacher and the boy, the boy looking such a lonely, helpless figure?

**

Shortly after entering Standard VII, I won a place at a Central school, soon to be opened. Nine years had passed since I had stood on the cork mat waiting for the nun with the nice smile, since when I had learnt reading and writing, the basics of arithmetic and most of all the importance of discipline, religion and implicit obedience. Science, Algebra, Geometry, Trigonometry and Mathematics were mere words having no significance, and I was into my twenties when I first heard the word matriculation. Like the other children of my generation, I had learnt to live in fear of priests, teachers, policemen and parents in that order, at the same time keeping an eye on the neighbours, who could be extremely hostile at times.

Whatever else may have been lacking in our education, we were never short of songs and ballads, some beautiful, some beyond our comprehension, but all sentimental. Old Blue Chin taught us 'Annie Laurie', 'My Braw John Highland Man', 'Logie O' Buchan', the haunting 'O Rowan Tree' and many others with a distinct Scottish flavour, the Scouse accent and the Scottish dialect making their rendering memorable. From Quirky we got 'The Golden Vanity', 'Jockey To The Fair', 'Tom Bowling' and a lovely ballad – 'My Lady is an archer rare/ and in the Greenwood roameth she/ there never was an archer yet that could compare/ in skill with my Laydee.' And how we enjoyed the rousing lines of 'The Mermaid':

One Friday morn as we set sail
I and our ship not far from land
We there did espy a fair mermaid
with a comb and a glass in 'er rand
'er rand 'er rand
with a comb and a glass in 'er rand.

As you'd expect, the Irishman gave us 'The Last Rose of Summer', 'Moira My Girl', 'The Emigrant', ('I'm sitting on the stile Mary, where we sat side by side') and somewhere along the way we picked up 'The Star-Spangled banner', the German National Anthem and the Russian 'God the All-terrible, Thou who Ordainest Thunder, thy Clarion and Lightning The Sword.' No wonder they had a revolution.

A little while ago I attended a Prize Day at a fee-paying high school where the children lined up and sang, 'I'm forever blowing bubbles.' Can you believe it, with all the lovely songs of the British Isles (and Ireland), that was the best the teachers could come up with. Next year, 'Hound Dog'?

On opening day at my new school I stood, one of a long line of boys, as the Archbishop, come to bestow his blessing on the project, swept past in a swirl of vestments and sanctity. An odd experience, it was the closest I'd ever been to a Holiness. The teachers wore shovel hats, soutanes and benign expressions, deluding us into thinking they might be more sympathetic than our previous overseers, a belief soon dispelled. The Headmaster, a head case in his own right, on his first visit to our classroom (form, please), delivered a lengthy homily and, waving a forefinger (of which the top joint was missing), announced that any boy failing to do his best would be pogged – an expression new to us but a clear threat given added emphasis by his remarkable resemblance to Lon Cheney.

Once regarded as bright sparks at our previous schools, my school-mates and I now competed with brighter sparks, who wore the sort of clothes rarely seen on our side of the tracks. The star turn wore a tweed suit, a bow tie and sported a real leather school bag, which impressed the teachers as well as us but unfortunately for the lad, he proved to be an idiot.

I shared a desk with a boy who was brilliant, but who steadfastly refused to help me with a difficult lesson until I had bribed him. I heard later that he had become a priest, and if I know anything then Gerry would finish right up there on the balcony with the Pope. Dress ranged from the aforementioned tweeds to hand-me-downs and worse. The boy sitting behind me, described by the English master as being so clever that further teaching was a waste of time, wore a threadbare gansey, boots almost beyond repair and a close-cropped head which had only one connotation for us: lice. I wonder where he finished up – the Docks most likely. Another lad whose father was a sea-going steward often turned up wearing a starched front, obviously his father's, something we might have charitably ignored except that it sometimes escaped from its moorings to curl up, exposing his bare chest. I never took to the school; the discipline was absurd, it had no status – not even of a secondary school – and being a good three miles away, with tram fares out of the question, getting there was a chancy business meaning three on each hand if you were late – no way to start the day.

Before long I was facing a crisis. The Headmaster, with scant regard for my feelings, informed me in front of the class that I was the only boy in the Form without the school cap (light blue dark blue panels) and to ask my parents to remedy this forthwith. My father was a non-starter, holding the view that such high-class education was not for the likes of us and in any case there was a job for me on his coal cart. My mother hesitated at the expense (the cap cost three and sixpence) but dear old Aunt Polly came to the rescue with not only a cap but a school bag. I had to pass through a particularly tough district on my way to school, hiding my newly-acquired cap under my gansey in case the local hard-knocks recognised it as a symbol of being on 'the other side.' This was a desperately poor area, even worse than that in which I lived but every year for one whole week it came alive. Banners and streamers hung everywhere, flags and garlands festooned the houses, all of them displaying a five-pointed star and pictures of a royal couple on snow-white horses. The inhabitants organised colourful processions, got drunk, sang their tribal songs and shrieked their hatred of the Papes. I saw all kinds of objects in the streets, including a crudely made confessional box and a side of bacon with a card attached saying 'Cured at Lourdes'. Shocked to the core, I described it to my mother: she thought it hilarious.

We were supposed to stay at the school until we were sixteen but, aware that I was approaching fourteen and old enough to earn money, my mother, probably suffering agonies of frustration, had made up her mind that it would be time for me to leave school, with me leaving behind for ever my school cap and bag – of which I was rather proud.

***

Without the pawnshop, half the local population might have died from malnutrition. Ours occupied a prominent position on the main road with its most important department, the Pledge Office, around the corner opposite our house.

Monday morning would see a queue of women clutching bundles wrapped in a pillowcase or a torn sheet. Inside were the huddle of customers smelling of sweat and unwashed clothes and above us rows of dark suits, dangling like victims of summary executions. I remind myself of my instructions: to ask for ten shillings, or failing that, seven and six, and should that fail, to bring the bundle back and try a more sympathetic establishment elsewhere.

Behind the high counter Mr Hodgson, wing-collared, clipped moustache, keeps the assembled throng firmly under control. 'Coat, vest and pants: seven and sixpence,' he announces briskly, glancing sideways to confirm that his acolyte has entered the details correctly on the pawn-ticket. Then, ignoring the plaintive cries of, 'God forgive you – it was ten shillings last week!' he slams the money on the counter as another bundle is presented for his inspection.

Anything capable of passing the rigorous standards of the Pledge Office is pawned: wedding rings, war medals, clocks, watches, suits, sacred statues, musical instruments, stewards' tunics and even the precious Lyndsay petticoats, which some women wore one, two or three at a time. Some articles were pawned week after week, their pledge value slowly eroding as they became familiar to the manager.

Each bundle is carefully scrutinised: a nicely laundered pillow-slip might contain nothing more than a collection of rags; a beloved statue, its chipped nose fixed with a little glue, invisible to all save the manager's eye. My own bundle might be father's long johns or my suit supplied by the shop round the corner, worn once and rarely seen again. Interest was sixpence a week for ten shillings and the office stayed open until 10 o'clock on Friday and Saturday.

Towards 10 o'clock, and depending on how benevolent the money-lender had been, my mother might try to redeem a bundle: Da's underwear or, exciting thought, my suit. At that hour the Pledge Office was eerily quiet, the only sound, apart from the low murmur of voices out back, was the purring of the gas jets, cocooned in their fragile mantles, their soft glow lighting the worn floorboards and the bundles crammed into racks lining the walls. Conscious of the corpses enshrouded in the gloom above me, I wait patiently until the acolyte appears, studies my pawn ticket and hands me a bundle. It's my suit. Tomorrow is Sunday. I can swank (modestly of course). Once, playing Newmarket with some mates and my suit having one of its rare outings, one boy turned back the lapel of my jacket, an action I barely registered until at home I found a pawn-ticket there. The memory of it doesn't make me cringe any more, but it did for a long time.

My mother persuaded the manager to give me a Saturday job, which meant standing from nine in the morning till nine at night (less one hour for dinner), guarding rows of second-hand boots, lined up on wooden benches at the front of the emporium. A length of string threaded through a lace hole of each boot was intended to discourage theft and I was reminded of this years later when I noticed that for exactly the same reason only one of each pair of shoes was displayed outside shoe shops. Lucky for me, such an idea was unknown in 1922 or the chance to earn two shilling would have been lost.

Mr Lyons, a mournful-looking man in charge of the second-hand clothing, the boots and me, had a withered arm which he held in his good one as if for consolation. He rarely smiled except to encourage a potential customer and then he allowed his features a faint quiver. He stood all day, silent, flat-capped, almost invisible behind his counter at the end of a narrow passage – the hob-nailed boots of generations of customers had hollowed out the floor boards into raising highly-polished knots. When my job as Keeper of the Boots became routine, it was a welcome relief to be sent to the Cocoa Rooms for a mug of tea and a fried egg on bread for Mr Lyons. The return journey was of necessity a slow one: poor Mr Lyons doing his twelve-hour stint in the second-hand clothing department must never have known the joy of a really hot cup of tea.

The Cocoa Room was a warm and welcome refuge, especially for early morning workmen, its bright lights shrouded in the haze of steam rising from a tea urn permanently on the boil. The menu was simple and unvaried; fried bread, fried egg and a steaming hot mug of mahogany-coloured tea. Choice of afters was limited to a Pudding Cake, a four-inch square concoction of raisins, currants, candied peel and the odd foreign object. Known as 'the docker's wedding cake,' the residue would be clinging limpet-like to your gums long after the rest had been persuaded to go down. One I bought at a Cocoa Room on the dock road (with the threepence I had avoided paying at the outpatients' department of the Northern Hospital by ducking under the paybox) gave me a twinge of anxiety when I regurgitated – and only just managing to do so at that – a short length of tarred twine normally used for securing orange boxes. Nevertheless, with a cup of tea served in a mug thick enough to cause lockjaw it was good value for money.

Now and then I was sent by Mr Lyons to his home – a two-storied Scotch house occupied by his own and three other families, one in the cellar. It was a squalid house in a squalid district through which I would later have to pass on my way to school and, young as I was, I realised why the poor man had so little to smile about.

The pride and joy of the pawnshop was the jewellery department, with its display of rings, brooches, watches and chains, many of good quality, having been bought in various parts of the world by local seamen. There were rows of war medals, medals of the Great War, the Boer War, South African war, the Zulu War, Malakand and other futilities.

This was my first wage-earning job and I was proud to hand over to my mother the two shillings I received for eleven hours of constant vigilance. The worst part of the job was seeing the other kids, happy and excited, hurrying to the cinema at three o'clock. After the last child had passed it took a while to shake of the feelings of rejection.

In an area dominated by the Church, birth control was unheard of and anyone advocating it would have and Mother church after his/ her blood. As a result, swarms of children had to be fed and clothed in this area, including the twenty-six produced by my parents and our immediate neighbours. For many people the pawnshop was a godsend, yet somehow a Hooray Henry in any British film of the day pawning his gold cigarette-case to pay off his gambling debts would earn people's admiration, whilst one of their own using the same service in order to exist was regarded with undisguised contempt.

CHAPTER EIGHT

Life on the Railways

I have no recollection of my last day at school, but my first at work is clear enough. Determined that I wasn't to join my father on his coal cart (one reason being that I wouldn't be paid), my mother found me a job in the city. Doesn't that sound grand? And in Drury Lane too.

The office in the basement of the India Buildings was occupied by the manager, a nattily-dressed Scotsman, and three young women, one being the secretary-typist on her Yost typewriter. I would listen in awe when she took the receiver off the hook and spoke in pure cut-glass tones to Daddy. My arrival at 8.45 am coincided with that of a horse-drawn railway van from which a little white-haired, bow-legged man (looking slightly startled when I called him sir after signing his delivery note) unloaded a large skip. I was well trained. When the skip was opened it revealed stacks of men's collars, beautifully laundered; high, low, soft, wing, all kinds and conditions of collars which were duly sorted out on to tables by the women. Most were for delivery by van. The remainder, packed neatly in cardboard boxes, were loaded on to the enormous carrier of a sturdy iron-framed bicycle and, a bit wobbly at first and with little idea of the addresses on the boxes, I pedalled off into the unknown.

There had been moments when I had hoped I would be an office boy, but it was not to be: I was an errand boy and had found my niche, my teachers not having prepared me for anything higher. Still, as I have already said, they did teach me some never-to-be-forgotten songs.

At twelve o'clock on Saturday I handed the sealed envelope containing a ten-shilling note, my wages for the week, to my mother, who in return gave me fourpence pocket money for the week. At this stage of my development a lot of her time was spent restoring the seat of my trousers which had frayed almost to extinction owing to the long hours spent in the saddle, my protruding shirt-tail causing much well-bred giggling amongst the young women in the office.

Having a day free from deliveries I was sent with the van driver putting leaflets through letterboxes in Formby. It was the first time I had ridden in a motor vehicle and a real thrill it was to ride through the city past our street, slightly marred when the driver, his black hair bouffant and corrugated, told me with a malicious grin that he had served with the Black and Tans. I knew little of that organization except that they were bad news for the Irish people.

Ever ambitious for me and believing I was worth more then ten shillings a week, my mother had a word with Aunt Polly, the beloved aunt who had rescued me from the indignity of not possessing a school cap. Her son was something in the Youth Employment Department of the Education Committee (a colleague was Arthur Askey) and in no time, hearing my name called, I stood before 'Uncle Harry', seeing the gleam of amusement in his eyes as he surveyed me in my new Melton overcoat, stiff-backed and nervous, remembering my mother's instructions to stand up straight and speak up.

Harry lived with his parents in a middle-class district with the pleasant-sounding name of Tuebrook, a place so quiet and respectable you could hear the grass grow. On the rare occasions I visited their home the sight of Harry in flowered dressing-gown and holding a long cigarette-holder looking like Owen Nares impressed me greatly. During the War he had been 'Commissioned in the Field', which meant that after all the officers had been killed or wounded Harry, as the senior N.C.O., was promoted to officer rank on the spot, thus enabling him to lead what was left of his men in further suicide charges against the enemy, a form of action popular with the Generals billeted some forty miles behind the lines.

Following this interview I became a telegraph messenger with The London Midland and Scottish Railway Company. The wages were fabulous, sixteen shillings a week less three pence for something or other, the job a dream. The vast station with its high-arched roof, the smell of burning oil, the sudden violent hiss of steam, the crowds pouring on to the platforms heading for 'the Cotton,' the Shipping Lines, the great Insurance companies, the Docks and the myriad organizations of our wonderful city were all there, as well as clerks, typists, messengers, managers and the professionals (First Class, blue and white upholstery, antimacassars). Trains roared in and thundered out to faraway places: Glasgow; Edinburgh; Hull; Leeds. Messengers carrying cotton samples, snow-white tufts in brown paper wrappings, dashed to place them on the Manchester trains, careful to avoid the electric trucks loaded with parcels.

The Excess Baggage man, his weighbridge piled high with luggage, studied the scales, the owners standing by exhibiting various shades of annoyance at being roped in. Tips were what made a porters life bearable but nobody ever tipped Mr Genovese, the Excess Baggage man.

Pausing to marvel at the dexterity with which a porter bowled empty milk churns on their rims right across the platform to a waiting colleague who caught and lifted them straight on to the waiting baggage-car without once losing the rhythm, I hurry to Main Line and Inspector Charlie Harrison with a backward glance at the rough wooden box lying solitary on platform seven, white-painted letters indicating that it was the property of H. Pierpont c/o Walton Gaol.

Inspector Harrison never spoke, he bellowed. From his tiny office where the station ended he controlled the passage of all steam trains in and out of the station, conducting a telephonic war with signalmen slow to carry out his instructions, cursing oil-stained shunters or exploding with wrath at some fireman dawdling at the turntable which reversed the massive engines. His rubicund features and Old Bill moustache were crowned by a straw boater which no official would dare to suggest that he replace with the regulation cap. Charlie always gave me a big welcome when I appeared with a wire at his office, little more than a shack, treating me with as much courtesy as he was capable of and I remember him with affection.

There were six clerks in the office, two messengers, a switch-board operator – Miss Ashcroft, the only female I would ever meet in an otherwise totally male environment – and a supervisor. Fred and Ambrose, though still young, were veterans of the recent War, the others a bunch of old fogies, mean and irascible. Newspapers cost a penny except *The Times*, which was twopence. To attract new readers, coupons for free gifts were given away, such as quarter-pound bars of Cadbury's chocolate which meant that, in competition with the porters, I was obliged to join in the scramble for newspapers left by the passengers and the clerks got very cross if those I brought back proved to be without coupons.

The worst one was the supervisor. who came from some up-country mangel-worzel parish, Rainford I think, plodding round the office in his ticket-collector's trousers, 'blue serge, hard-wearing, last a lifetime,' his sour-puss expression relaxing into an Uriah Heep smile as he recounted a chance conversation with the top-hatted stationmaster referring to him as 'Mesther'. A creep if I ever saw one.

He gave me neither training nor encouragement, speaking to me directly just once when he informed me that I had failed my clerical examination. George, the lad I was replacing, gangly and unsmiling, was a railwayman from the shine on his highly polished boots to the crease in his ticket collector's trousers (clear indication that he was well-in). Shewing me round the various departments, he was often asked, 'How's your Dad?' from which I gathered that 'Dad' was a railwayman, which mine wasn't. In later years it became a question I was to hear with dismay, knowing that if it was a choice between me and a 'How's your Dad?' for the smelly fish dock or toilet-cleaning or something equally unpleasant, then it was me for the short straw. The office was available to the public and if a clerk was in good humour he would let me pull the switch which whooshed the telegram enclosed in its jute cylinder down the pipe to the G.P.O. on the other side of the city. One regular was an alderman and magistrate who telegraphed ten-pound bets, a quite legal process and very different from our back-street bookie, John Henry, taking penny bets from the locals. He was constantly harried by the police who used all kinds of subterfuges to catch him, including disguising themselves as women (when not doing this they were terror-izing the peaceful, Mah-jong playing residents of Frederick Street in Chinatown).

The junior ticket collectors in their smart double-uniforms aroused my envy. As potential clerks we were not given uniforms, so I persuaded a kindly guard to give me one of his old caps; though it threatened to part me from my ears I wore it with pride, ignoring the snide remarks it invoked.

On Grand National Day (Friday), the station heaved with racegoers heading for Aintree by electric train. On the steam side all was relatively quiet and it was here that I came face to face with Prince Monolulu, resplendent in a feathered head-dress that depicted the Prince of Wales' crest, his skirt and poncho a riot of colour. He was a black man, a tipster, famous on every race-course for his cry of, 'I gotta horse.' Seeing him on the wrong side of the ticket-barrier, instinct told me that the Prince (who I assumed was from Moss Side) was fare-dodging but, unimpressed by my official cap, he gave me a smile like a row of grave stones and a tip, St Hilda's Cottage. It lost.

Came the day when I said to my mother, 'I haven't to go to work tomorrow – we're on strike.' Whatever her reply was, the following day I set out for work with my carrying-out tucked under my arm. Nobody had told me which side I was supposed to be on and approaching the pickets, Johnny Southern and Teddy Guy, I was feeling nervous. However, they listened patiently as I explained that it was more than my life was worth to return home. They let me pass, which is how at 15 I became a scab.

One of the young clerks had joined the strike: he would be transferred when it ended. Another victim comes to mind, a young Cockney fireman, still in overalls, transferred from his London depot to work as a porter, desperately keen to talk to anyone, even me, and hopelessly out of place in a Northern environment. Having nothing to do, I wandered round the station – past the deserted cab rank, waving to the pickets, past the tearooms with their bright lights, tea urn and hubbub of conversation shut off for the duration. In the Porters' Room the iron kettle hung empty and rusting over the ashes of a fire that was never allowed to go out, not even on Christmas Day. The tracks, freed from pounding wheels, lost their metallic gleam; a door banging somewhere sent a jarring wave of sound throughout the station and when an Inspector by the name of Morgan attempted to take a train out it was so heavily stoned from bridges that further attempts were abandoned.

After it was over, at least for the railwaymen, the scabs and I received a letter, a remnant of it which I still possess, which states: 'And to inform you that as a small recognition of the part you have played, a grant of nine days standard pay will be made to you. The occasion is one of great importance in the history of constitutional government of this country and I will shortly send you a suitable certificate placing on permanent record your service in the hour of the nation's need. Yours faithfully, H.G. Burgess' (note that 'standard pay' touch: they might have stretched it to time and a half).

Five years later, on my twentieth birthday in 1931, they made me redundant and I clean forgot to remind them of the vital part I had played during those nine fateful days in the Hour of the Nation's Need.

Not that it would have made much difference: when it came to redundancies the 'how's your Dads' weren't even on the list.

Messengers worked shifts, 8 am to 5 pm and 6.30 pm to 2.30 am. It was the late shift which was to prove my undoing. At half-past five the clerks swanned home, leaving one of them on duty until ten when he too departed and I was left on my own. Sometimes the switchboard needed attention, a woman perhaps asking for someone in the station hotel. I put her through then listen in: 'Darling I can't hear you – you've gone faint!' I flick the switch to neutral. The Morse instruments, disturbed by some magnetic force, would set up an appalling clamour. The first time it happened I almost ran home. I wander on to the station to watch the 10.17 from York bustle in then the Edinburgh express from which, when all is clear, the dining-car attendants wheel out skips, piled with the carcasses of chickens and similar delicacies to a dump at end of the platform where, almost before they have had time to get out of the way, scores of rats appeared from under the wooden ramps, fighting and squealing over the juicy scraps.

The last train pulled out, good-nights were shouted, the night porter pads across the concourse past the silent booking offices and the shuttered bookstall, stopping to check the padlock on the Tea Rooms, then disappearing under the archway beneath the station clock, leaving in his wake lights dimmed or extinguished. Around midnight the lads from the goods stations came, ramming bundles of invoices in their bright yellow envelopes through the pigeon-hole shouting their place of origin as they did so: 'North Mersey, Canada Dock, Huskisson, Waterloo, North Docks, Gt. Howard Street!' When all were safely gathered in they were placed in a canvas bag to be handed to the guard on the 02.25 train, a ramshackle assembly of vans, coaches, and wagons which clanked its way into the heart of Lancashire bound for places such as Rochdale, Swinton, Atherton, Pendleton and New Hey, towns blazing with the lights from scores of cotton mills.

It was inevitable that the time would come when I would fall asleep, and when it did I woke with a start in time to hear the whistle of a departing train. Grabbing the canvas bag I tore on to the platform only to see the red rear light of the 02.25 fading into the black night. The night-porter was there seeing it off. 'Missed it?' he said enquiringly and for the first time I saw his face, a dead ringer for Bela Lugosi. I thought of the dozens of clerks, pens at the ready waiting for invoices which would release tons and tons of goods: you'd have thought the misanthrope on nights would have wakened me if only by a bang on the window, but no, I was doomed. I would have to take the rap. It was a subdued lad that trudged home that morning along a deserted Scotland Road. And so to bed. In the bedroom my mother sits by the fire nursing the last of her eleven children, a weak sickly child. I try to get him to smile but without success (he lived to survive being torpedoed twice). We talk for a while in whispers so as not to disturb my father. I make no mention of my earlier mishap before climbing into bed to lie at the opposite end from my ten-year old sister who sleeps peacefully, the horrors of school still some six hours away.

In the corridor of the head office in Manchester where I had been sent to be disciplined, the prospect of facing my mother should I be sacked had me deeply worried. There were others waiting to be seen, some white-haired, heads bowed, speaking to no-one, their faces revealing an awful anxiety. What crimes had they committed, I wondered.

My inquisitor, representing the Company in all its majesty, sat behind a desk, with his highly-polished boots, butterfly collar, bowler hat (crowning symbol of authority) and gold medallion dangling from his watch-chain, which gave him access to all parts of the system, all combining to make me feel deeply apprehensive. We stared at each other for some time, which didn't help matters. What he said I don't remember: I suppose he read the riot act. I came away sweating, but relieved that I still had a job.

It was not unusual coming off the late shift to be stopped by a policeman and asked what I was doing abroad at such an hour and it took a while to convince him that I was a bone-fide citizen, albeit a young one. Sometimes I walked home along the dock road, but having witnessed, along with a patrolling policeman, a horde of rats crossing from one building to another, I decided to keep to Scotland Road. The bobby had seen this sort of migration many times and he told me that the rats always knew when a fresh cargo of grain had been unloaded in the building they were heading for. Not that Scotland Road appeared to be any healthier. On one occasion I couldn't believe my eyes on seeing what appeared, to my young mind, to be a Red Indian in full warpaint – feathers, moccasins, tomahawk, the lot, padding silently past the Morning Star on the other side of the road, glowing cigarette clutched between his fingers and clearly defined in the darkness. I ducked into the shadow of a street lamp and to my relief he padded on. Later I read that four genuine 'Indians' were performing a tribal dance on the stage of the Trocadero cinema to accompany a Western called, *The Flaming Frontier* and the mystery was solved, but look at it from my point of view, I ask you. What chance would a four-feet ten-inch lad in short pants have had against the tomahawk of a Comanche Indian?

* * *

I was fifteen, life centred on work and the wages it brought in. Joey, Gongy, Chuck, Nippy and Henny, now wage-earners, could still be found queuing for the children's matinee on Saturday afternoon where all was Cowboys and Indians, Charlie Chaplin and Tarzan. The nearest library was some two miles away right in the middle of Proddy Dog country, so with the music teacher being the sole possessor of a wireless set, it was left to the cinema and the gramophone to provide us with culture. For the music lovers, the songs coming from the United States via Woolworths sixpenny records (three songs on each side) seemed to concentrate on those Americans who had got over their wanderlust and were returning home to places with romantic names: West Virginia; Carolina; Georgia; Wyoming; Tennessee; Nebraska (I'm going back again to Ol' Nebraska an' if anyone should ask ya etc.) and 'Swannee, how I love ya, how I love ya, my dear ol' Swannee' (wherever that might have been). The British responded with, 'I'm going back to Imazaz, 'im as 'as the pub next door.'

'Moonlight and Roses' was a great favourite with us and the squeeze-box merchants played it on every occasion: weddings; funerals; christenings and the occasional 'do,' whilst on the serious side we listened with due reverence to John McCormack, Count of the Holy Roman Empire, singing, 'The Rose of Tralee' and similar ditties. Our parents, when they sang (which I'm afraid wasn't very often), clung to the songs of the Music Hall, by now virtually extinct: 'My Rosary'; 'Golden Slippers'; 'If Those Lips Could Only Speak' (you couldn't hear this without weeping); 'The curse of an aching heart' and a favourite of my mother's, arising from the German bands that toured the streets before the First World War and were believed to be spies:

Has anyone seen a German band
German band, German band?
I've been looking around all
  upon my own
I've searched every street so
  near and far, near and far
  ja ja ja
I want my Fritz to play tiddly bits
On his big trombone.

My sister and I bought a portable gramophone for three pounds ten shillings on the weekly, the salesman assuring us that it had a Gerrard motor and was therefore the best. No doubt thinking we needed a spot of culture, he threw in two free records, one featuring Tchaikovsky's 'Chansons Sans Paroles', the other 'The Broken Melody.' This had a heart-stopping moment which never failed to bring a lump to the throat when the music stopped for a few seconds due, we were told, to the sudden death of the violinist's mother.

The Church continued to dominate our lives – Mass on Sunday, sometimes twice, Benediction in the evening and again on Thursday, Confession on Friday when, if we couldn't remember any sins and so as not to waste the priest's time, we invented them (mild ones of course).

The Newsreels gave us our only glimpse of the doings of royalty and the upper classes. Apart from the odd launch by Queen Mary, royalty seemed to spend most of their time at the races in the company of Lord Lonsdale and Lord Derby (how that man must have fed: he was mountainous) or The Aga Khan, all, as you would expect, suitably dressed in shiny top-hat, frock-coat and spats. It was rumoured that the Aga Khan had himself weighed in gold every year, which must have impressed his followers washing their smalls in the Ganges.

No launch was complete without Queen Mary and I have often thought how much better it would have been to let a shipyard apprentice perform the ceremony. He would have taken the memory of it to the end of his days whereas I'm sure that on the way home when George asked Mary the name of the ship she launched that day Mary would say: 'How do I know? I'm forever launching the things. I can't be expected to remember all their names.' You see my point.

We accepted without question that royalty and the upper classes along with our teachers and priests never used bad language, told dirty stories or indulged in furtive fumblings. Such activities were to be found only amongst the working class and in war time it was right and proper that we should be led by officers from the upper classes, who would be described as gallant whilst the soldiers were merely brave.

Having failed to become a clerk it was time to say farewell to the crabby old men, to the late shift and to Fred and Ambrose, those young-old war veterans. Fred on the late shift told me stories of the War and the horrors he and his comrades endured slogging their way in retreat through Ypres where, 'there wasn't a brick left standing,' he said, 'it was just powder.' In another war I remembered Fred when passing through Cassino, Italy, a town in a similar state.

Time to say goodbye to the bustling city station, now no more, and the sign, high in the roof which announced, 'They come as a Boon and a Blessing to Men, the Pickwick, the Owl and the Waverley Pen,' which inspired me to blow my first week's pocket money on a Venus pencil costing all of fourpence.

* * *

So I found myself at a pleasant suburban station as a Junior Porter, uniformed, being introduced to a large flat high-wheeled handcart from which I would be expected to deliver parcels to a community of some thirty thousand souls.

There were cartons of K shoes, rolls of carpeting, Palethorpes sausages, cans of film (Tom Mix, Lillian Gish, Dolores Costello, Ramon Navarro), dogs in cages, cats in cages, pigeons in crates, strawberries in crates, two thirty-pound bags of fish on Thursdays for the convent (the ice from the straw bags soaking my trouser leg), gramophone records and car parts. There were Hoovers and Slazenger racquets for the professionals who wanted me to share a cup of tea but I never had time. Then, time to be sitting on the shafts of the handcart eating my dinner; a twelve-ounce can of beans, cold, three bananas, half a dozen thick slices of bread (my carrying-out) and a couple of lemon-cheese cakes, still hot, donated by the auburn-haired supervisor of the bakehouse where I delivered cans of Foucard's frozen eggs. The bananas were a penny each, no selling by the pound then and the pork was delicious.

The bowl of sweets on the chemist's counter looked inviting and I was told to help myself whilst he retired to sign my note. When he returned my cheeks were bulging and it was fortunate that I knew the precise location of the Gents in the district: the sweets were Ex-Lax.

It was arduous work roped to the handcart, straining against ice in winter, melting tar in summer. Once, making no headway on a desperately icy road, a black limousine drew alongside and the occupant jumped out, calling to his chauffeur to come and give a hand. Between us we managed to get going, the chauffeur telling me in a low voice that my helper was Sir Bertram Hayes, captain of the ocean liner *Majestic*.

Those were the days when every station had its station master, trains were clean and ran on time (mostly). Snow, fog or ice slowed them down but rarely brought them to a standstill. Spotless waiting rooms and equally spotless toilets at a charge of one penny were taken for granted and passengers were often reluctant to leave the cheerful fires in waiting rooms which greeted them on winter mornings. Station Masters were gods, ours was no exception. His warm padded overcoat, gleaming polished boots, the gold lettering on his cap all proclaimed his exalted position, backed by a moustache whose length would have aroused the envy of an Austrian Archduke. He was unaware of my existence until one unlucky day, attempting a short-cut with a fully-laden handcart, I failed to negotiate the subway beneath the station, which was where he found me. So there I was caught in the act, the Archduke, moustache quivering, demanding an explanation, his expression alternating between fury at me to sweetness and light at irate passengers squeezing between my handcart and the subway walls.

This station employed seven clerks, two foremen, two junior ticket collectors, three porters, a lampman, a cleaner and me. The Goods yard, requiring the services of a Goods porter and two of the clerks is now a car park, the Baggage car no longer runs. The twice-a-day London train, three coaches pulled by a steam engine joining the Lime Street/Euston at Edge Hill, ceased operating years ago and you can pass through the station a dozen times a day and never see a railwayman. Station Masters have departed with the Dodo.

At Christmas and summer holidays Rosalind, Elizabeth, Robin and Jonquil sent their tuck-boxes and luggage home from college and university to be collected, transported to the station and delivered to any part of the country for two shillings. It was known as 'Passengers' Luggage in Advance.' Two civilians with a thirty hundred-weight vehicle were employed for this purpose but now and then I would be called upon to take the odd trunk or two which had been overlooked. There was always a tip, sometimes as much as a shilling and I remember with a hint of nostalgia how easily I heaved many a brass-bound trunk on to my shoulder and carried it to the attic at the top of the house, followed by the maid imploring me to be careful and to mind the banisters.

Despite their size those houses had a homely lived-in feeling and, although I rarely saw them (it was all beribboned maids who answered the door), the people in them were quite friendly.

George Fisher, the chief clerk, insisted on my handing over to him any tips I made: at the end of the week he gave me whatever I had made with strict instructions to hand them over to my mother.

Meanwhile the higher-ups at Head Office were giving me trouble, refusing to give me a travel pass on the grounds that Liverpool was not a residential area, which might be news to the three-quarters of a million people living there at the time. Thus, faced with the prospect of having to pay my fare each day I decided not to, trusting to my uniform to see me through the collector's barrier and feigning sleep when ticket inspectors boarded the train, an unnecessary subterfuge as I was so exhausted at the end of the day that I fell asleep immediately on settling in the train.

***

One dreary evening, with the mournful dirge of the foghorns drifting in from the river, I arrived at a newly-built house with a parcel containing a small carpet. Getting no reply I assumed that the potential owner had not yet taken up residence. So, wet, tired and hungry I did the unthinkable: I forged the delivery note, stuffed the carpet into the brand new bin at the side of the house and promptly forgot all about it.

It must have been some weeks later that I was called to the office where George Fisher was talking to a gentleman. 'This is Mr Moon,' he said. 'He's enquiring about a carpet which should have been delivered to him. Do you know anything about it?' As the saying goes, it all came back to me. After they had both got over the shock at learning how I had disposed of it, George suggested I had better go with Mr Moon and, 'see if it's still there.'

Off we went in his car. It was still there. What blessed days those were. Today the carpet would have long disappeared complete with the bin. George squared things up with a tolerant Mr Moon and I was saved from a further and possibly final confrontation with the bowler-hatted nabobs of Head Office.

Eventually it became too much and after two years during which I lost neither a parcel nor a wheel, I was replaced by a motor vehicle. Quite often I left my handcart with its little cargo for a few minutes and never was anything stolen from it nor was I ever cautioned to beware of thieves. People were so honest those days.

I remember the new-type Lindbergh train, its compartments weighted down with brake blocks, tearing through the station at eighty-five miles per hour, the steamship Lochmonar homeward-bound from Canada breaking its back on the revetment in the Crosby channel in 1927 and a wide boy flogging some of its cargo on the station (enormous salmon for a shilling). Winter and fog and the plate-layers were called out during the night to man the braziers beneath the signals which stopped them freezing up. The sons of the local gentry, clad in their sharp suits, bowler hats and furled umbrellas, gathered by the bookstall laughing and joking before heading for Liverpool and 'The Cotton', amongst them young Taylor, popular with the station staff because he shewed no 'side'. I watched him from my lowly position, such an elegant young man and one to be envied. Some fifty years later, quite by chance, I read his obituary.

Passenger Guards were supplied with uniforms of good quality serge, double-breasted jackets and braided peaked caps. They were expected to keep their trains to schedule and never, ever to upset the passengers. Their working hours were any eight between 5 am and midnight. They were paid sixty-five shillings a week and they spent every night in bed.

The uniform of Goods Guards was the same rough cloth as worn by signalmen, who like them were hidden from view of the public. Porters too wore the same but they were of no account, on view or otherwise. They also were paid sixty-five shillings a week, reporting for work at bizarre times like 2.03 am, 4.46 am, and 12.13 am and they rarely spent a night in bed, which may explain why, with a few exceptions, they were such a crusty old bunch. To ensure they didn't over-sleep, the Company provided a guard-caller to wake them up at an appropriate time. This was my new job, one requiring neither training nor intelligence. It was also permanent nights so that in winter I saw little daylight. Working from 10 pm to 6 am I made ten calls, walking to each one and waiting for my knock to be acknowledged, usually by a snarl or a grunt from a bedroom window or the other side of a front door. To say I was an unwelcome visitor would be an understatement.

CHAPTER NINE

On the Dole &
On the Docks

> 'Once upon a midnight dreary,
> as I wandered weak and weary …'
>
> E. A. Poe.

It was 1928 the pubs closed at ten o'clock on the dot, working class nightclubs had yet to be invented and no sixteen year-olds were to be found walking home alone. Apart from the Bobby on the beat, an occasional coggy watch-man and myself, the streets were hushed and empty. If there was time to spare before my next call, instead of returning to the marshalling yards, I made myself as comfortable as possible in a shop doorway, aware of the approach of the policeman checking the locks on the shops. His rubber-soled boots made no sound but his conversation (with himself) could be heard loud and clear. Cinder Lane petrified me. On the corner stood an abandoned mansion, a poster in one of its windows warning off trespassers (at least I think that's what it said, I never got near enough to read it) and looking so much like a ghostly face that it took a real effort to pass it. When a full moon shed its pale glow on the rows of gravestones in the nearby cemetery, only the fear of being sacked (and my mother) stopped me from turning back altogether. Although seventeen, I hadn't yet rid myself of a belief in banshees, ghosts and all things supernatural. The Church, Saturday afternoon cinema and a lively imagination must take the blame for that.

After a year of this I was promoted to Number Snatcher, spending the night in clogs and oilskins trudging between endless lines of wagons recording the number and destination of each wagon, the purpose of which was never explained to me. It was always dark, always raining and there were rats as eager to sample the contents of the wagons as were the railwaymen. I would be startled out of my wits when a bulky figure looming out of the darkness turned out to be a railway policeman hoping to catch the thieves. When the shunters became aware of his presence they sent wagons hurtling towards his hiding place causing thunderous crashes as buffers met buffers. The hapless Bobby must have felt terrified.

All night long the goods trains, fifty and sixty wagons long, shuddered to a halt, smoke and steam issuing from every crack and fissure of the massive engines. Shunters ran forward, pinning down brakes on the leading wagons until satisfied that the train held. The Inspector instructed the fireman to unhook the engine which then departed for the shed. After that gravity took over. Each wagon, unhooked from its neighbour, was guided into a road by a shunter manipulating the brake with a length of stout timber called a sprag and when, as sometimes happened, a wagon got away from a shunter because of a broken sprag or faulty brake, the shunt engines dotted round the sidings set up a continuous popping of their steam whistles as warning to look out for the runaway. Such a one screeched past me at umpteen miles an hour hurling itself and its load of red sand high into the air when it met the points at the end of the Grid. An awesome sight.

I was eighteen, earning twenty five shillings a week, a good wage for the time. At twenty I would be on the maximum for a Porter of forty shillings a week, the lowest wage for uniform grades and one which, like all other grades including drivers (ninety shillings a week) and firemen, remained the same up to the outbreak of the war and beyond. If and when it improved I was no longer a railwayman.

However, it seemed I was never to achieve such giddy heights because at twenty I was made redundant, the fate of most of the lads reaching that age despite having spent all their young lives on the railway, confident that they had a 'job for life.'

I went to work as usual on the eve of my twentieth birthday and during the night, control told the Inspector to remind me that my time was up, which Harry did. A dyed-in-the-wool railway-man, Harry would have had no qualms telling his mother she was redundant if it had ever been necessary. There was nothing in writing, no goodbyes, no 'Best of luck son,' and at 6 am I slithered down the well worn path from the sidings to the Aintree road and into the Depression.

It was January 1931. For my mother, who had spent most of her married life trying to 'make en's meat', it was a cruel blow – like most young men of the time I had given up all my wages to the home.

On Monday morning with my mate Joe, also ex-railway, we joined the flat-capped, four-deep dole queue, shabby clothes giving off the odours of gasworks, tanyards, breweries and chemical plants. In the cobbled street men proffered *The Daily Worker*, *The Blackshirt* or *The Greenshirt* but there were few takers: newspapers were now luxury items. Entering the Dole office my heart sank at the sight of the queues at the various boxes. A board suspended from the ceiling advertised a lone vacancy for a Scammel engine driver. I joined the queue indicated by the initial letter of my surname, shuffling slowly forward until reaching the counter where a blue serge suit, white collar and pince-nez inducted me into the routine I was to follow for the next six months: Monday, Wednesday and Friday, ten-thirty sharp, Box Five. Failure to attend would mean loss of pay, no excuse for lateness, and most importantly, I was to declare any money earned since my last visit. Failure to do so was a criminal offence.

When on Friday I signed on, I was given fifteen shillings. l noted the figure 161 in a square in the corner of the signing-on pad. A veteran dole claimer explained that it represented the number of days for which l was entitled to the dole. It had started at 168. l was already seven down. Being on the dole was something to be ashamed of even though you were not responsible. The comedians of the day cashed in with songs like, 'He's Signing On', sung in dirge-like fashion. Another declared from the stage of a Northern theatre, 'Some young men don't intend to work: hundreds are saying so and millions are thinking it.' He himself had no problems about work, getting a thousand a week dressed in a kilt and singing Scottish songs in an exaggerated accent. It's a pleasure to report that he was soundly booed. Everyone seemed to have heard of the extraordinary individual who, despite being on the dole, smoked heavily, drank even more heavily, went to the cinema, the dogs and football matches, had a family who never went short, 'an 'im on the dole.' Of course he never existed, but it salved people's consciences to believe that he did. An irate Colonel wrote to the *Daily Telegraph* that he had *actually seen working-class children buying ice-cream* and the Government should reduce taxes for the middle-class so that they could employ more servants and so reduce unemployment.

Listening to the six o'clock news was a national habit and to say, 'It was on the wireless,' was to guarantee its unquestionable truth. So when we heard that Ramsay MacDonald's National government had decided return to the Gold Standard (whatever that was) because he was finding it difficult to balance the Budget, we hadn't got long to wait for what was coming. The dole was cut to twelve shillings and sixpence a week. Someone pointed out that this was only two shillings and a penny per day and what were we supposed to do on Sundays – starve? – but he was quickly put in his place: Sundays were included. Thus we were reduced to one and ninepence a day. Ironic to think that this was brought in by the Labour leader of the day.

Joe and I tramped the streets with little hope of finding work: we knew nothing but the railway and there were hundreds of people skilled in all kinds of jobs and trades prepared to do anything for a chance to work. My sister's boyfriend, who worked for Cunard, told of a trans-atlantic liner arriving in Liverpool with only a handful of passengers and the Chief Engineer being informed on its arrival that he could accept either the position of Watchman on the ship, which wasn't going anywhere, or face redundancy. He settled for the job.

We teamed up with a budding entrepreneur as door to door salesmen selling tea. 'Cathedral Tea', it was called, implying some connection with the Catholic cathedral to be built some time in the future. Armed with the names and addresses of all the Catholics in the neighbourhood, our Leader gave us a final briefing and we set off. The first call was nearly enough for Joe: he took one look at the Leader, hands held in an attitude of supplication, the precious packet of tea an inch away from the nose of a bemused housewife and collapsed in helpless laughter. 'Me do that?' he said, 'Never!' It took a little while to persuade him to at least have a go and we tramped those ugly, grey streets knocking on doors which opened to reveal sleepy-looking unwashed women or their husbands, bare-footed, unshaven, braces dangling, faces pictures of grim hostility. At the end of the week we arranged to meet in a pub to split the takings but our Leader failed to arrive.

The Docks were good for an occasional day's work, twelve and six a day union, ten shillings scab. It meant bribing some individual to get you a union card costing one pound and fourpence. This had to be negoti-ated in a pub and even if you were successful, there was the risk of being ordered off the dock by a union delegate despite your newly acquired union card. Raising the money was impossible. Australia, Canada and the U.S. had closed their doors to immigration With twelve million unemployed and soup kitchens a feature of the big cities, America had its own problems:

> l knocked at the door
> and I asked for some bread
> and the woman came out
> and said the baker is dead.
> Allelulia I'm a Bum
> Allelulia Bum again
> Allelulia put his hand out
> to revive us again.

We talked about stowing away until we heard of the conditions in the Las Palmas gaols where most of the stowaways ended up. It was never a good idea; Joe and were just not the tough, resilient types prepared to take on such hardships. One of our mates did make it though, not only getting to New York via a trimmer's bunk, but succeeding in finding employment with the Brooklyn Gas, Light & Coke company, as well as making a few dollars on the side delivering bottles of Prohibition hooch to customers of a small-time gangster.

The day came when the pencil was drawn through the final seven days of my dole. The next step was an appeal to the Public Assistance Committee. The interview was brief. Having taken all the circumstances into consideration, viz. my Father working, my sister working, the decision was that there was sufficient money coming into the house to maintain me and the family – no assistance would be given. l remember rising from the wooden bench and remarking rather desperately that this was the sort of treatment that made Communists out of people. A mild roar arose, one member saying, 'When you've seen as much of the world as I have …' I didn't wait to hear the rest, tottering out onto Stanley Road with the numbing realisation that I was now penniless. What I had experienced was the Means Test in action.

My father was an itinerant coalman driving his weary nag down dreary streets announcing coal, one and nine a hundredweight, followed by a rival coalman bawling coal, one and eight. More than once I was sent to ask Dave the blacksmith to shoe the horse on tick until the day when he sorrowfully refused: my father owed too much. My sister worked at the Dunlop Rubber company bringing home six-inch squares of partly-processed rubber blocks, soaked in bitumen, which had to be separated into thin strips, smelling awful and leaving our hands covered in the stuff, which defied all efforts to remove it. It was piece work and the pittance she received and my Father's income, such as it was, according to the experts at the P.A.C., was enough to keep a family of six. It wasn't.

While you were on it, dole money was yours to do whatever you wished with but P.A.C money, which could go on indefinitely, was for food and lodgings only. Many schemes were devised to beat the system, like claiming you had left home because of overcrowding, or had been kicked out by an irate father (not uncommon this). Then on the promise of say, half a crown a week (25p) an acquaintance or a relative living in a nearby street would agree to tell the P.A.C. visitor when he called to verify your claim, that you were living under her roof. During daytime it was easy to explain that the lodger was out looking for work, but a knock on the door at ten o'clock at night could reveal a woman asking to speak to Mr Lodger. Should the 'landlady' unwittingly blurt out that he was at the pictures or, heavens above, in the pub, then retribution followed. You were hauled before the P.A.C. to explain such criminal behaviour: it was, 'How long has this being going on?' P.A.C. money stopped immediately, and possible prosecution of you and the landlady was just for starters: after that all that was left was the Parish, which gave food coupons only, never money.

A P.A.C. visitor called on a family in receipt of relief and enquired as to the number of people living in the house. On being told four, he suggested that the five chairs they possessed were more than enough and told them to sell one.

As usual, the heroines of the day were the women facing up to outbursts of rage and frustration from bewildered husbands, deprived of the jobs and the pay packet which gave them self-respect and the satisfaction of knowing they were maintaining their families. They continued to wash, scrub, sew and mend and perform miracles of house-keeping with the measly pittance which was their husband's dole money.

Beer was fivepence a pint but could be had for fourpence if you were prepared to look for beer such as Joules Stone Ales. There were kiosks which sold cigarettes, ten for threepence halfpenny, Capstan

Full Strength, Players Navy Cut and Ardath. Woodbines and Player's Weights were five for twopence. Cork-tipped would never have been tolerated. Passing Clouds were oval-shaped, scented and combined with fish and chips could make you violently sick, as I discovered. Smoking was a badge of manhood. Few women smoked and those who did were considered brazen.

Men and women wore the same clothes year upon year. At Burman's on Scotland Road, men's suits were sold at twenty-one and fivepence, coat, vest and pants one colour: brown. When it rained, large patches of Indigo dye appeared under the armpits, a clear indication to the locals of its origin and the reason for the belief that an umbrella was given out with each suit.

＊

Ballroom dancing, or jazzing we called it, was all the rage, featuring the Waltz, the Fox-trot, the Slow Fox-trot, the Quick Step, the Veleta, the Paul Jones and the Empress Tango. A good dancer was the equal of a good footballer and in the big dance halls the semi-professionals were idolised.

The dance hall we patronised was a room over a shop. The owner's wife sat in the doorway entering each name and the entrance fee, sixpence, in a ledger. The men dressed for the occasion, wearing their Burton' fifty-five shilling suits, wide lapels and padded shoulders or the more expensive sixty-five shilling ones with wider lapels and more padding in the shoulders. The wearing of collar and tie was strictly enforced. Bowler hats were normal headgear and to see a burly docker hang his bowler hat and furled umbrella on the coat stand supplied for that purpose evoked neither surprise nor derision.

The girls bought their dresses through Clothing Clubs organised by local pawnbrokers, paying a shilling a week to the Tally Man and on Friday night very attractive they looked as they circled the floor to the opening number, 'Keep Your Sunny Side Up', on the three piece band – piano, violin and banjo. Any girl refusing a request for a dance, even if the 'feller' was reputed to have two left feet, would be asked to leave by the M.C. That was Harry, the owner, a tall, cadaverous war veteran who found breathing difficult, having been caught in a gas attack some time during 1914–18.

The highlight of the evening was the 'Ladies Excuse Me', when those men targeted by the women would he asked to dance and the whispered, 'Can l take you home?' was agreed to by the girl. The man's ardour however, would slowly evaporate with the girl's repeated assertion as they hurried through the darkened streets that 'Me Dad'll be waiting on the doorstep!' and he was. Eleven o'clock was, of course, very late.

Many a romance blossomed in the sweaty atmosphere of Bullen's Dancing Academy and I have fond recollections of one particular wedding – the beer flowed copiously, the guests overflowed from the little two-up two-down into the street and, joined by the policeman on the beat, they danced into the early hours. The wedding feast was memorable, made on the premises, as much as you could eat, spare ribs and cabbage – delicious.

CHAPTER TEN

Blackpool, Big Bands, & Seeing Stars ...

Things began to look up for Joe and me when we were put on the list of summer porters and when the railways became busy we got telegrams instructing us to report for duty at certain stations. The lucky ones got mainline stations where tips could be made; others got wayside stations where loading wagons in the Goods yard was part of your duties and hard work it was. I spent two summer seasons at one such station, cycling twelve miles to get there and leaving at 4.30 am The station master, the foreman, the lampman and a porter lived in the village a mere half a mile away but it was me who opened up the station, lit the fire in the porter's room (the sole means of hot water), issued tickets, swept out and met the first trains in. That was the way things were done on the railway seventy years ago. On the opposite shift was Orlando, another summer porter who lived in Walton.

The station was open on Sunday, two trains in the morning, two in the evening. I left home around 8 am to meet the first of the trains due at 9.20, followed by the other at 11.30. I stayed on the station until the last of the two evening trains had departed, arriving home some fifteen hours after leaving. Only the hours spent on duty were paid for. Those spent in between trains didn't count, so my remuneration for the day was six shillings and eightpence, which was double time.

One Sunday morning, when flicking back the catch on the window of the porter's room to let in some fresh air (it always stank of rotting vegetation), the sash window crashed down on my fingers. Unable to free myself, I looked over the top of the window in the hope of seeing a farm labourer or the village bobby on his rounds but it was the Sabbath and the chances of seeing anyone were remote. Down the line I saw the signalman empty a bucket of water from the steps of his box and I shouted, waving my free hand. He gave me a cheerful wave back and went on inside. There was a train due on the downline platform furthest from where I was trapped so I continued to shout until the signalman finally saw me, got the message and pried me loose. It was all very painful for me but he thought it hilarious and no doubt entertained the locals in the local hostelry with his version of it for many a night afterwards.

Sam, my foreman, was regarded as a character with a particular hatred of 'townies'. He had a long sad face, a drooping, tobacco-stained moustache and eyes the colour of oysters. His uniform hung on his bony frame, the hem of his jacket caressing his knees whilst the back hoisted itself high enough to expose his braces. A skeleton finger would point to some object on the platform and an unintelligible snarl would fall from his lips. It was days before I was able to translate the noises into normal speech. The price of a pint could buy his undying loyalty for a day but I had other things to do with my money.

Thus, on late shift he wouldn't allow me to catch the last train home, which left at 11.28 at night, two minutes before my shift finished at 11.30 pm, leaving me to make the long bike-ride home through the pitch darkness of the countryside, finally emerging to the welcome sight of the street lights of Fazakerley and its tram terminus.

Having to get up at four o'clock, it was inevitable that one morning I would sleep in. Thus, twenty minutes behind schedule, I arrived at the station, which lay about six miles from my own. Abandoning all thoughts of the country lanes, I carried the bike across the line and continued my journey, pedalling madly on the narrow stretch along-side the track. The station finally came into view, the dwarf-like figures of the passengers, ticketless and no doubt very annoyed, clearly visible. A distant rumble, a hasty glance over my shoulder and there it was, the first train, throttle wide open, coming hell-for-leather. I pedalled even more madly and, as it bore down on me, I scrambled off the bike, thinking I would be sucked under its wheels. Regardless, it tore past in a clamour of wheels, pistons, steam and smoke, a fiendish shriek on its whistle warning me out of the way – or was it the driver indicating his joy at beating me to the station? I'd lost the race. Drenched in sweat, spattered with cinders, I pedalled slowly on. The old signalman leaned out of his box. 'Tha's late lad', he said. How right he was.

A townie at heart, the countryside was source if wonder to me. Rabbits for me were either quite dead and skinned, or caged in hopeless captivity in someone's backyard, but here they lived with hares and stoats, crows, pheasants and birds the like of which I had never seen. Wild strawberries grew on a bank behind the porter's room; a farm labourer gave me a capful of eggs laid by ducks in their secret places and an old countryman offered to bring me a remedy for a sore throat, dog fat, to be rubbed in. When next we met I was relieved to find that he had forgotten about it, or perhaps he had run out of dogs.

There was an air of peace about a wayside station in the late evening. Few people got on or off the trains and only at weekends was there any activity, when the locals travelled to the nearby towns to let their hair down, the climax reached on Saturday night when the joyous prospect of a sleep-in on Sunday morning gave sanction to their getting drunk at all stages from tipsy to paralytic. On certain evenings the station master would be seen hurrying on to the station carrying a small attaché case and exchanging his warrant for a Privilege Ticket before boarding the train. Someone remarked that he was off to the Lodge, a matter of little interest to me at the time until some years later when the station master at Blackpool South, a pleasant old buffer, told me why he could expect no further advancement (the ultimate advancement including Top Hat and Tail Coat). Of the twenty station masters, he said, representing the stations between his and Liverpool, he was the only one who was not a Mason. It became clear why those station masters I had worked under all wore such a smug air, a sort of, 'you can't touch me' attitude and well they might, for at that time Red Lodge No. 197 was the spiritual home of the chairman of every major railway company.

* * *

In 1935 I was made a permanent member of the railway company, uniform provided, able to earn two pounds a week, every week, to work Christmas Day and Sunday (double time), Bank Holidays and Boxing Day (single time), to get up at four a.m for early shift and get home any time after midnight from late shift. It meant that I could become, after many years, a ticket collector, guard or signalman and after a staggering number of years an Inspector. The first step along this road was to become a Leading Porter. Such a post was advertised in the thirties when the new Old Roan station was opened. The incentive to apply for this was a shilling extra per week and the competition was fierce. At the other end of the scale were the drivers, the aristocrats of the uniform grades, earning four pounds ten shillings a week which reflected in their attitude towards us on the platform: one of amused contempt.

I had spent a summer at Blackpool as a temporary ticket collector, thoroughly enjoying the noisy night life and it was a pleasant surprise when my application for transfer was agreed to, although not to Blackpool itself but to St Annes, a very elegant affair, employing two full-time ticket collectors.

The passengers were the crème de la crème, amongst them the Assistant General Manager of the L.N.S., Ashton Davies, boarding the 08:30 London train, which took him to his office in the capital. (At the last count he was a prominent member of four Lodges). The Club trains stopped at St Annes to pick up the Cotton men going to Manchester, female attendants alighting and relieving them of their overcoats and briefcases, then shepherding them onto the coaches which, with cushioned armchairs and antimacassars, were simply drawing-rooms on wheels. Those were the days for some.

It was my good fortune to make friends with a railway clerk to whom I owe a great deal. Tommy was a self-confessed hedonist, perpetually cheerful, showing me cafés, restaurants, theatres and places I would normally be nervous of entering. As a clerk, he was entitled to six free rail passes a year. I, being uniform grade, was allowed three and and we made good use of them. When my allocation ran out Tommy, through 'someone I know' would arrange for another free pass to be issued. It was all rather mysterious but I didn't ask questions. London, Edinburgh, Paris, Ostend, Belfast – we savoured them all years before they became clogged with holiday makers and rip-off merchants. We took our annual leave in the off-season. London was magic with lights everywhere, Lyons Corner Houses and the nippies, the long drawn out cry of 'Evening Standard!' from the newsboys, the Tower, (entrance half a crown which we considered a bit stiff) no queues, stroll round at leisure, chat with the Beefeaters, watch the antics of the ravens, browse the Caledonian market where everything for sale lay on the bare cobble stones, with no stalls.

l picked up six books, which cost sixpence the lot. Amongst the signatures on the flyleaf of one was that of Major Atlee. We sat for three hours, minus intervals, on wooden benches at the Old Vic to watch a performance of Hamlet in modern dress with Alec Guinness as the lead. Wonderful. I don't know where the Old Vic was, or is, but coming out I remember seeing directly across the road the Express Dairies, my only sense of where I might be.

And then we saw the Café Royal: luxurious red-plush seating, a Press photographer shewing me startling pictures of the Spanish Civil War then tearing Spain apart. The law said that the serving of alcohol after 10 pm was illegal, so you bought a sandwich with each drink which made it legal and allowed you to drink in the Café Royal all night if you wished. We paid three shillings each for a seat in the Centre stalls at the Prince of Wales theatre (theatre going was very expensive those days in London), bemused at the shrieks of incredulous laughter which greeted the comedian parodying the BBC weather forecaster when he said, 'and the weather forecast, bloody awful.'

We visited the Mint where, before our very eyes, two shilling pieces (florins) were made and deposited in a shower on to a swift-moving conveyor belt where a gimlet-eyed operative picked out the flawed ones, sensing what we were thinking for, without glancing up, he picked out a coin and handed it to us for inspection. The guide shewed us the flaw. At the end of the tour I offered the guide a tip, tentatively, thinking it might not be the thing to do in such a grand establishment, but he grabbed the half crown with both hands, explaining that the work at the Mint was only temporary. Asked what he did when not employed at the Mint, he replied, 'I work on the roads, road-mending.' On one of our visits to London, Tommy was given an invitation to visit Elstree to see the filming of, *Knights Without Armour* with Marlene Dietrich and Robert Donat. For some reason we didn't go, a matter of some regret. I'd loved to have seen the Blue Angel in the flesh.

Ostend gave us our first taste of the Continent: the word 'Apothecary' over a chemist's shop, red mullet in the fishmongers, hardly enough flesh on their transparent bodies to fill a hollow tooth, the pillboxes on the sand dunes, relics of the Great War. When Tommy was taking photographs of these, I detected someone darting between the dunes ducking down when he thought he was spotted. It was winter, the holiday makers had returned to their homes and we must have been the only strangers in town and here we were being tailed. Perhaps they thought we were spies and with another war no more than three years away, why not?

At a hotel, The Manchester, we called in for a cup of tea served from a teapot in which hung a limp and exhausted tea bag and from which no amount of repeated dipping would produce anything resembling tea, much to the waiter's annoyance. We stayed for two nights in a pension where the proprietor's daughter amused herself by grabbing my hand and shoving it up her jumper whilst her mother looked on, smiling benevolently. I learnt the correct pronunciation of Knocke and Zeebrugge and at a dance hall where my British-style dancing was a minor sensation, my partner said that no Belgian girl would dream of dancing with a Walloon, which fortunately I wasn't. From her remarks, I gathered that they regarded the Walloons as some form of primitive life.

Passing through the customs shed, the man in front of me had more than his duty free allowance of wine, so the officer, learning that I had nothing to declare, gave me the surplus bottle, which I then gave to the man on reaching the other side of the barrier. What a pleasant gesture, I thought. Would it happen today?

It was dark when we arrived at Dieppe from Newhaven. The lone Cook's man attending to the few passengers coming off the *Prince Baudouin* not only spoke French but excellent English, we thought, until we discovered that he was English and happy to keep us entertained talking about himself. When he fell off the ladder and broke his leg whilst following his trade as a painter a decorator, it meant a long spell in hospital during which time he had taught himself French to such a degree that, on discharge, he applied for and was accepted by Thomas Cook as an interpreter. Nobody in my experience had ever achieved any thing quite like that and I thought it a remarkable story.

Apart from that, my abiding memory of the train journey from Dieppe to Paris was a visit to the toilet and having to hang on grimly to two straps suspended from the ceiling, straps provided to help you maintain your position on the lavatory as the ancient train swayed and rattled its way towards Paris. At times, I found myself suspended in the air with nothing beneath me, hilarious but worrying. Arriving at the Gare du Nord, we walked into a brightly-lit café and ordered coffee and something to eat. It was 5 am and we were on the Continent.

The franc was, from memory, 178 to the pound and we found a neat hotel just off the Rue de Rivoli, calling in for breakfast at W.H. Smiths café, above the book store, where I couldn't take my eyes off a French officer straight out of *Beau Geste* who sat motionless, holding both hands of his female companion to his lips and gazing unblinkingly into her eyes. So romantic, so French.

At some time a girl attached herself to us, Catherine Pascallion, her self-appointed mission to protect us from being overcharged, for, as she explained, all English visitors were known to be wealthy and easy meat for certain establishments. She hadn't met any railwaymen on free passes. The Dome café, which Catherine favoured, was crowded but with Catherine as our guide we got seats and she pointed out various characters, amongst them a Monsieur Haakova, the darling of Paris, she said. It took a while for me to realize that the darling was none other than one of our Saturday heroes, Sessue Hayakowa, pronounced with the emphasis on the 'yak,' Liverpool style. He was the Japanese colonel in *The Bridge over the River Kwai.* The Dome, I read somewhere, was a favourite haunt of the Duke of Windsor. If it was I didn't see him …

We drank red champagne in the Latin Quarter, three francs a glass and we didn't question the colour because we'd never seen the real stuff. Each drink was brought on a saucer with the price indelibly marked and at the end of the night the waiter rattled the the pile of saucers together and told you the amount. The Latin Quarter was a disappointment: we had expected to see evil-looking Apache dancers and wild-eyed volup-tuous women like Lupe Velez but it was all rather quiet. We came across a number of British lads on their way to fight on the Republican side in the Spanish Civil war (the recruiting office was in Paris) and as a member of The Left Book Club I might have been expected to join them, but it required a commitment and courage which I didn't posses.

Down a grubby side-street at an equally grubby Box Office we booked seats for the Folies Bergère, one place we had to visit. People who prob-ably had never been there had said with many winks and nudges that it was a place not to be missed. And here we were reaching eagerly for the opera glasses available for a five-franc piece from a slot in the rear of the seat in front. True, the bare-breasted chorus girls had us sinking lower into our seats but in no time we ceased to be impressed, I suppose on the basis that having seen one you've seen them all.

The highlight of the show was a real spellbinder. It opened with a scene of convicts in striped jerseys lying on the floor of a prison ship on its way to Devil's Island, all displaying signs of tortured sleep. Through the bars of the brig appears the face of a beautiful girl who opens the door and steps in, treading her way softly between the recumbent figures, singing in a low voice that lovely song, 'Night and Day,' at which the doomed men cry out the names of their loved ones whom we know they will never see again, 'Jeanette! Fifi! Delphine!' Very moving it was.

At the Pam Pam, a bar on the Champs Elysée, playing Poker Dice with some Americans, I ran clean out of francs and the barman lent me five hundred francs, which I promised to repay the next day (and I did) refusing to take my watch as security when I offered it. Not much, you might say, at 178 to the pound, but almost a week's wages to me. Nor should I forget that Tommy received two tickets through one of his friends for the annual ball of the Barmen of Paris at the George V Hotel, one of the swank events of the year and why we didn't go, I cannot say. Perhaps he flogged them as we were running short of cash.

* * *

Some fifty five years later, my son took myself and my wife to Paris in celebration of our golden wedding. The teen-age grand-children who came with us dominated the trip (as well they should, I hasten to add), as teenagers would anywhere. Ice cream and pop were priorities, and the opportunity to visit ancient haunts had no chance. It was July, the Champs Elysée was crammed to the pavements and we couldn't keep up with the others so me and the wife stopped for a drink. I ordered a pint and a half of beer and when the bill came it was seven pounds fifty and the waiter was looking for a tip. Ripped off, cheated, fleeced and gobsmacked we were. There was no Catherine to save me from these vultures: she was gone, gone with the Pam Pam, the opera glasses, the Barmen of Paris, the lovelorn officer. Night and Day would never again make the charts, red champagne would never again be available at three francs a glass, saucer and all. No, he didn't get a tip.

We got to travel around Britain as well. In Edinburgh, in the Palace of Holyrood, we saw the blood stains, still fresh, left on the floor by Riozzi, secretary to Mary Queen of Scots after his murder by the Queen's husband Lord Darnley and his mates. They stabbed him fifty-six times so there must have been a lot of blood there in 1566. The guide conceded that the stains may have been renewed from time to time but of that he wasn't sure and he directed our attention to the secret staircase leading to the Queen's bedchamber which was more in our line. Otherwise Edinburgh was a cavern of gloom. At night time nothing stirred apart from ourselves and a couple of likely-looking body snatchers. There was one night spot, the Havana, but reluctant to dive into the darkness of the city's wynds we gave it a miss and had an early night, waking the following morning to one of the best breakfasts I've ever had. Good for you Edinburgh.

Jean, a girl from Belfast with whom I had been corresponding, invited us to her home where we were treated with typical Northern Irish hospitality. They enjoyed the conviviality of the pub and we were only too ready to join in, which is why we found ourselves in Owen McGinty's pub on the Antrim road. The original intention was to shew us the beauty of the Antrim road by car, but soon after leaving the city a pub came into view and by common consent it was agreed to pay it a visit. This was about two in the afternoon and we left Owen's about two o'clock the next morning. I have a vague recollection of attempting to play darts and of a confusion of people phoning their friends in Belfast to come out and join us, which they probably did, for the place was, in modern parlance, jumping. Of the beauty of the Antrim road we saw nothing, although later on with Jean I did see it as well as the Giant's Causeway. We strolled along the banks of the Lagan and looking back, now I think it's a crying shame that such a beautiful place should be so divided with that pointless-of-all-divisions, religious strife.

The barmen in the pubs in the dock area were skilled in the art of pulling a pint then hurtling it along the metal-topped counter to land precisely in front of the customer. Women were not allowed in pubs alone, but in the company of a man they were accepted. Women in the company of other women were allowed to enter pubs but were then herded into a corner which had the ambience of a confessional box.

Jean's mother, a lovely, happy person, took us to the Grand Central Hotel on Royal Avenue where we witnessed the coffin of Lord Carson being conveyed on a gun carriage to its last resting place, having been brought by destroyer from England. Both sides of the avenue were lined with crowds and every few yards the Royal Irish Constabulary stood with carbines reversed, eyes alert, scanning the surrounding buildings for the ever-present threat of trouble. That day I saw grown men sobbing and felt quite literally the tension in the air. Jean's sister was 'going out' with an RUC man and when he called one day, his whole appearance was one of menace. I was transfixed at the sight of the revolver he carried, and when he heard my Irish sounding name I'll swear he gave his gun pouch an involuntary hitch. What a way to live.

In Italy during the war, when a concert was organised in the squadron (the turns provided by the men themselves) one would-be performer was forcibly reminded of what would happen to him if he sang Mother MacRee, a song beloved of Republicans. The freedom we were fighting for didn't extend to the freedom to sing some maudlin Irish ballad.

In summer, Blackpool entertained six million visitors, most of whom came by train. During 'Wakes' Week,' whole towns closed down and the operatives headed for Blackpool to stay in the same boarding houses in which they had stayed for year after year, greeted with embraces and kisses by landladies who knew their Christian names and every vice and virtue of which her guests were capable. The food they got was the same as they got at home but here they were waited upon, the ultimate luxury.

I shared a room in a boarding house with the landlady's son, a workmate, and as the season progressed we were moved from room to room ending up in the attic, where the sloping ceiling posed a constant threat should you suddenly start up in the night. I recall seeing the old girl in her kitchen crooning over the `digs money' left by departing guest and being startled by the venom in her voice as she whispered, 'They haven't gone yet,' referring to some people who were shewing a reluctance to leave. Gone was the sweetness and light of the previous Saturday.

Blackpool was marvellous value for those with little money. As well as the promenade and the piers, three of them, there was the Tower and its magnificent dance floor with Reggie Dixon at the Organ, all for a shilling. Even better was The Winter Gardens: here, also for a shilling, you could see a first-class show then dance till eleven. On Wednesdays at eleven the big bands appearing at The Palace would take over and we danced until one o'clock in the morning. Jack Hylton, Geraldo, Ambrose, Lew Stone, Henry Hall: they were all there and with Dutton's beer at fivepence a pint it was sheer heaven. After the last waltz on Friday night when the dancers streamed off the floor, to those girls who had not found the romance their minds and bodies craved, came the realisation that this was the last night, the last chance and the Romeos lining the staircase knew it and took full advantage. 'All dolled up in glad rags – tomorrow may turn to sad rags.' The most popular eating establishment, which served 'more than you can eat' helpings of fish and chips for sixpence, was owned by an avowed Communist. At the end of the season Pablo took his entire staff for a week's holiday to Paris. A workmate, Alan Andrews, drove an MG Midget which cost him £38 and we rode to Stanley Park where we attempted to play golf, one and sixpence a round, ninepence during Scotch Week (which was actually a fortnight.) There were tragedies: two sisters fell out of a plane belonging to Alan Cobham's Flying Circus and a young man jumped off the Tower, crashing through the the roof of the Ballroom, the inquest recording that he couldn't get on with his grandmother.

There was money in Blackpool and at some time or other we saw all the stars of the day on the station: Tom Mix (ask your Grandad) an imposing figure even without his six-shooters, Gracie Fields, shooing her Dad and others of her family through the barrier, George Formby, Dougie Wakefield, Wilson Keppel and Betty. There was Paul Robeson occupying a third-class carriage with his white secretary, asking me not to bring any more requests for autographs, Leopold Stokowski chasing Ann Harding, a most beautiful actress appearing at the Grand, Yvonne Arnaud, who came to do, 'French Without Tears,' Jacob Epstein giving me a winning smile and a tweak of the fingers as he handed me his ticket.

***

At the station where I worked as a Ticket Collector (we were engaged for the Summer reverting to Porter status when the season ended) the concourse was always thronged with people wanting information and unable to get near the Enquiry Office. The porters when asked would solemnly aver that it was forbidden to give any information whilst the Enquiry Office remained open. The exchange of a few coppers would then produce the required information. There were queries of a different nature like the granite-faced miner who sidled up to me to ask in a gravelly voice, 'Wheer's stone?' meaning where's the piss-stone or, 'Can you direct me to the gent's please?' A working knowledge of dialects was helpful.

We had our own characters like Les, a porter who never smoked, swore, drank or played cards and still possessed a great sense of humour.

Whenever tipped by old ladies, he would see them safely berthed in a compartment then return with a cup of tea for the old dears. If ever a man was squeaky clean it was Les. In later years he would become a member of Parliament. Then there was the woman who approached the ticket barrier, retreated a few steps and came back, this time carefully avoiding the spacings between the paving flags. If she thought she'd touched one, she'd go back and do it again. Dante the magician usually departed on a Sunday morning in his own private Pullman, plus seven tons of equipment and a with a very generous flourish of tips. Because of my mate's insistence on sitting in the front row of the theatre, we saw how some of Dante's tricks were done which spoiled it for me.

At such close quarters I felt almost sorry another comedian who lay full length on the stage, his head almost touching the footlights, his face a mask of sweat as he tried desperately to put over his act: he was billed as Tommy Trinder.

Evening excursions cost one and sixpence (7p) return and brought thousands from all parts of Lancashire. Most came for the dancing, though some went no further than the nearest pub, emerging legless at closing time no doubt to enthral their mates on Monday morning with an account of the marvellous time they had on Saturday night in Blackpool. One day, the station was put on full alert for the arrival of the chief financial boss of the railway whose name I cannot remember. According to the Press, he was one of the financial experts advising the German Chancellor, Herr Hitler. l wonder how he felt when the balloon went up.

Come September and the ending of Summertime, the railway would have no further use of my services and the Dole queue again become the focus of my existence but I would never forget those lanes along which I rode in the early morning, of those long-ago days, hedgerows smothered in blossom, finger posts demurely pointing the way to my destination, the flock of wood pigeons rising in alarm, all this to be destroyed one day to make room for a soulless bypass.

CHAPTER ELEVEN

Bombers Over Liverpool

So, it was a lovely sunny September morn, a Sunday, and I was sitting on a luggage truck, when I heard Mr Chamberlain's announcement over the loudspeakers that we were at war with Germany. The Duty Inspector sent me to the Enquiry Office to help out, besieged as it was by hundreds of holidaymakers anxious to get home. My first enquiry was from a lady wanting to get to Rosyth (a place I'd never heard of), where her son was in the Navy. Only after a lengthy trawl through the time-tables was I able to give her some sort of advice. As all regular services had been replaced by emergency services, I have often wondered if she got to see her son that day.

Answering an appeal for Goods Guards, I applied, and was trans-ferred to the sidings where I had spent a portion of my youth. Maybe that explains why one day there I was, seated in the brake van of a goods train (destined for the Liverpool docks) which was stuck in a tunnel, the driver having very sensibly come to a halt to avoid the attentions of the German bombers overhead. The muted hiss of steam from the engine and the reddish glow of the tail lamp on the tunnel wall were my only companions, and I began to wonder why I had exchanged the care-free life of Blackpool for the blackness of a tunnel in Liverpool; not to mention twenty wagons chock-full of explosives.

If there is a turning point in anyone's life, mine came one morning when, filling in my timesheet, l was joined by a guard due to retire at the weekend. In contrast to most of the guards he was a quiet, pleasant fellow, and I remembered when guard-calling he would invite me into his house where, on the wall of the kitchen, was a photograph of himself and other soldiers taken outside an estaminet somewhere 'behind the lines' in France. The wonderful men who could give meaning to those words are all gone, the horrors they endured, the agonies they suffered.

The place where we did our clerical work was a stone-flagged white-washed room – little more than a large cell – lit by a single gas jet bearing an instruction to turn down the gas before leaving. There were no toilets, no washing facilities: you went home in your muck. The old railway guard gazed around him. 'I wish I'd never seen this place. I wish I'd never seen the bloody railway,' he said, with such vehemence that, hearing it, my mind was made up. It was no place for me either. I was getting out. I knew the consequences: my white card evidence of a reserved occupation that made me immune from call-up would have to be surrendered, but the old man's outburst was enough. What remained of my life wasn't to be given to any railway company.

So, to my mother's great disappointment and ignoring the clerk's malicious, 'You'll have to go into the army you know', I gave in my notice, got a job in a factory and waited for my call-up.

After the grim rosters of the railway, it was sheer heaven to work eight to five, to have every Sunday off and sometimes, despite the war, whole Saturdays off. Then there were the girls. From the age of fifteen my working life had been spent in a totally masculine environment, and when girls approached me (I was in the Stores) I blushed. It must have been a novelty, for at any time of the day there were pretty girls hanging round, apparently there to witness my blushes. Needless to say, I married one of them, Marie Furnivall.

***

German bombers were busy over Merseyside, the docks being their obvious target. The biggest and most important of these was the Gladstone. On the other side of the road, immediately opposite the dock, was a pub, the Cradock, of which it was said that more German spies were served there than customers, which perhaps had a grain of truth in it. With Joe, my brother-in-law, who was a dockside electrician, I walked on to this dock unchallenged.

Joe showed me around one of the fifty destroyers, 'sardine tins', given to the British by the American government. Also in the dock that day was a battleship, a large Merchant Navy vessel and an aircraft carrier, *The Braham*, which had limped home with a massive hole in her chain locker, the result of a torpedo meant for amidships. Talk about security.

Our house was a mere ten minutes' walk to the docks, so when the

German bomb aimer pressed the tit just that bit too soon, my mother and I stood rooted to the floor as the entire window and brickwork of the kitchen crashed on to the newly-laid table for tea. Terrified and covered in dust, we made our way to the cupboard under the stairs until the 'all-clear' went at about 4 am. At 6 am, a warden ordered us to move out as there was an unexploded parachute bomb in the next street, so we hurried round to my sister's house which was still intact. I went to work as usual but got permission to return home, hoping to sort something out, and it was then that my mother said she had forgotten all about my brother who, as far as she knew, was still in bed. I tore round to the house, now roped off, and, after explaining the situation to the warden on guard, was allowed through. There was no sign of the boy so I abandoned the search, stopping only to pick up an official-looking envelope lying amongst the rubble. We later found my brother sheltering with other kids in the cellar of the Gaumont Cinema, being entertained with sweets and ice cream by a kindly manager.

The envelope contained my call-up papers. I reported to the recruitment centre in a bit of a sweat, as, according to the date on the papers, it was two days overdue. However, my explanation was accepted without comment and by none other than the same pince-nez and serge suit that had processed my first dole application.

So then to Padgate to be interviewed, photographed and uniformed. Shuffling along in a queue of civilians, we watched with some trepidation an airman on his knees, sleeves rolled up, plunging his arm to the elbow into a pool of stagnant water, from which he retrieved lumps of sodden paper. Was this some form of punishment or was it staged for our benefit as a warning of things to come? At the interview it was decided that I was to be an Armourer, immediately filling my mind with visions of suits of armour, pikes and halberds, although my instinct told me that this was not quite what the Royal Air Force had in mind.

Just three days after arriving at the training camp at Weeton, I got seven days' jankers for smoking in the classroom, making me something of a hero amongst the twenty-four sprogs with whom I shared a hut. Some even got out of bed to help me with the various straps and webbings before going on defaulters' parade at 6 am: boots and buttons polished to perfection, cap at the correct angle. A hurried breakfast and then we were marched off to school to sit and listen to the instructors, a blasé lot, droning on and on for hours about rear seat levers, retaining pawls, volute springs and similar gadgets. Only by a massive effort of will was I able to keep my eyes open.

My neighbour at the evening defaulters' parade wore an Observer's brevet, but no stripes, which marked him as a regular, a pre-war airman. Out of the corner of his mouth he informed me that he was 'from Warfamstow,' (Walthamstow), and that when the Sergeant asked if there were any Catholics on the parade I was to make it clear that I was one. The Sergeant duly acknowledged my profession of faith and we were instructed to clean out the church on the camp. The old sweat immediately took charge, instructing me to get two buckets of water which he sloshed down the aisle, after which we mopped up, and as far as he was concerned, that was it. Beckoning me to follow, he disappeared behind the altar and there in cushioned armchairs we regaled ourselves with cigarettes, a stack of newspapers and the altar wine. What remained of my Catholic upbringing was rather shocked (although more concerned at the prospect of being caught), but the one-time observer calmed my fears, assuring me that the Sergeant would never come in the church as he was 'one of them', meaning a Protestant.

The German bombers were operating over Merseyside apparently without retaliation, and when I got a letter telling me that my parents had not been seen for some days, suggesting they might be casualties, I found it hard to concentrate on the course. A sympathetic Sergeant sent me to the Adjutant to ask for leave. The Adjutant was a ten-bob-a-day Pilot Officer ex-schoolmaster whom I had once met when walking up the whitewashed gravel path leading to his office. On that occasion he had waved me imperiously out of his path. He refused my application, commenting that it was my own fault for living in places like Liverpool and Manchester, a statement which in all innocence I repeated to my Sergeant. His reaction was dramatic. I was called before the Training Officer, a Flight Lieutenant, who, convinced of the truth of my story and obviously furious, ordered the Adjutant to give me unlimited leave until I had found my parents, which must have made Pilot Officer Goddard, adjutant, ex-schoolmaster and would-be Caesar, severely depressed. It was two days before I found my parents, living in a communal air-raid shelter and having lost a second home, but unharmed. In 1947 in digs in Derby, my landlady, recalling the war days, told how her husband Bill, on hearing the German bombers going over, would come in from the garden to announce quite categorically, 'Liverpool', or 'Manchester'.

She was rather proud of her husband's ability to name the bomber's target, adding, 'He was a bit sorry when they stopped coming'.

I was now an Armourer, 'a GD with his brains bashed out,' as one cynic put it, posted to various stations in England; the high spot being Lindholme, where the station commander's wife, a glorious blonde, operated from the back of a Bedford truck at break-time, handing out enamel mugs of tea and rock-canes accompanied by a dazzling smile, to the gobsmacked airmen. The low point was Moreton-in-Marsh, parading at 6 am on a freezing winter's morning whilst an officer waggled a torch up and down our tunics to make sure the buttons were polished. To add insult to injury we were again inspected in the armoury. The pits.

There was an occasion I remember – when I was returning from leave, when the train I was on was stopped at Birmingham. The MPs directed me to a YMCA hostel to get a bed for the night. At the reception desk were three white American soldiers and a lone black soldier. The receptionist explained to one of the white soldiers that space was limited and he might have to share a room to which he agreed, adding, 'Providing it's not with this black bastard', indicating the soldier standing next to him. Never had I heard such a blatant insult, nor possibly had the receptionist, who blushed furiously then, staring him straight in the eye said, 'You'll take what's given to you or find somewhere else', at which the Yank subsided into a nervous snigger. I was proud of that girl.

Going overseas had a great attraction for me and when the chance came to replace a sick airman, I was quite happy to take it. So to Blackpool to be kitted out, with tropical gear, pith helmet, iron rations (a bar of chocolate, in a Gold Flake tobacco tin which required the use of an axe to make any impression on it) and brand new kit bag. Wherever our destination was it was obviously hot. Thence to the excursion platform of Blackpool Central Station, the very place on which I had sat one bright September morn and heard Mr Chamberlain say his piece. The porter (Dick Moon) locking the compartment door expressed astonishment on seeing me and answered my hurried enquiry with a whispered, 'Liverpool.'

And there we sat, anchored in the Mersey for two days before departing, destination still unknown, and leaving all we knew behind. Life would never be the same again.

Epilogue

Algiers was the destination of the ship; its task was to fight with the 8th Army to clear the Germans and Italians out of North Africa. The men marched across the desert enduring heat and thirst, flies and snakes. They slept in tents shared by six men sleeping on the floor were and the nights icy cold. They complained a lot about sore feet and bad food, and they often went hungry. But that was the least of their worries, of course. There were bombings, there were diseases, and many among them never returned home.

From Algiers they marched through Tunisia, and on a transport ship were taken to Italy where they saw the devastation that had been left by the departing armies. Ordinary men who knew nothing about war – who in some ways thought they were off on an adventure – saw horrors that they could never have expected; horrors that they could barely talk about when they got home.

My father, like many, learned much from his wartime experiences, good and bad; an ordinary man from Liverpool, once a kid from Scotland Road, experiencing things that would mark his generation forever. But he was lucky and he survived.

The end of the war was finally declared while the men were still in Italy. After four and a half years away from home, my father was demobbed and everyone thankfully returned to civilian life.

The Liverpool they returned to was not the city they had left. It had been severely bombed during the war with parts of it completely devastated and with many people having lost their homes. Those old neighbourhoods where my father had spent his childhood would never be the same again. The city where there had been work building aircraft and ships for the war was a changed place. There was massive unemployment.

My father had been away four and a half years, and like the others, had to adjust to post-war life. He had a young wife who he had left behind and they needed to make a future. He found work in the Midlands, moved there and they began a family, and a new life.